EXISTENCE & CONSCIOUSNESS

EXISTENCE & CONSCIOUSNESS

A Theory of Naturalistic Idealism

Richard James Lucido Ph.D.

EAST DETROIT EDUCATIONAL PRESS
Maple Forest Michigan
U.S.A.

Published by East Detroit
Educational Press
2603 Babbitt
Maple Forest, Michigan

ISBN 13:
978-0692825037

ISBN 10:
0692825037

Printed in the United States of America

Contents

What are the Constituents of Reality?   1

Doubting the Objective Presence of Matter   26

The Essesential Nature of Matter and Energy   38

Idealism Explains Quantum Mechanics   55

Consciousness is Existential Being   76

The Basic Workings of Naturalistic Idealism   91

Mental Causation   110

Speculations on an Idealistic Cosmology   123

Empirical Approaches & Concluding Thoughts   132

Appendix   149

Bibliography   153

1

What are the Constituents of Reality?

To say the world is an illusion is an over statement. That is in fact not what I mean. However, I would like to convince you of the absurd sounding idea that the primary constituent of reality is not the hard stuff of matter, energy, and space, but rather that there is no space, and that reality consists only of the interplay between consciousness and information. There are many reasons to seriously consider this idea, which expressed in various forms is nearly as old as recorded thought itself. Some of the reasons go back hundreds or even thousands of years, however most of the ideas that you will read here are much newer than that, and many are original to the present work.

As a younger man I would have laughed at this book and tossed it in the trash by the end of the first paragraph. At that time I thought that everything was physical. My dream was to be the first to discover how the brain made consciousness, how the movement of molecules resulted in my experiencing the smell of bacon, the painful crescendo of a burn, or the sound of a C#m. I would have regarded the preceding thesis as veiled religious dogma or, worse yet, mystical new age nonsense. I would have flippantly levied the charge that the idea was "unscientific" and would have considered it no further. I would have been wrong.

Being trained as a scientist (I hold a Ph.D. in psychology) requires one to develop a deep respect for the principle of empiricism, the idea that theories should be derived primarily from observable evidence. This is the hallmark of science. It is what separates it from philosophy and religion. However, of equal importance to this is the acknowledgment that science is predicated on certain assumptions, one of them being the idea that the physical universe is independent and self-sustaining, that it persists through time whether or not there is someone there to witness it doing so. This is not something that science has "proven" to be true, or even something for which it has accumulated direct evidence in support of. Rather, it is an *a priori* commitment, something that is assumed to be true at the onset, before any data is collected. Since it is impossible for an enterprise to prove the assumptions on which it is based, from the insular perspective of science we may never be able to neither prove nor disprove the thesis that reality is comprised of consciousness and information rather than matter and energy existing objectively in space.

Although at this time we may not be able to design an experiment to fully test this hypothesis, it would be wrong to conclude that science has nothing to contribute. In the 21st century responsible philosophic inquiry needs to be consistent with the accumulated body of scientific knowledge. A theory about reality that does not respect the empirical facts that science has provided about reality is fatally flawed. In the end it all has to fit. All the facts need to be consistent. That being said, a marked distinction can be made between the empirical facts of science and their contemporary interpretations. In other words, being consistent with the empirical facts of science does not mean taking as gospel the interpretations of the scientists who are discovering these facts. Interpretations (i.e., theories) are the result of the combination of empirical facts and assumptions. By having different assumptions one set of facts can yield more than one logically valid interpretation.

This book will question the validity of science's most basic assumption about the nature of reality. Namely, that physical things are in themselves self-sustaining, that they exist independently of consciousness. In the absence of this assumption, I hope to demonstrate that the empirical facts of science lead most parsimoniously to the interpretation that reality consists of the interplay between consciousness and information, that existence is primarily mental rather than physical.

Exploring Your Metaphysical Options

In addressing the constituents of reality philosophers typically recognize four general categories: materialism (all is physical), idealism (all is mental), dualism (there is both a mental domain and a physical domain where one cannot be reduced to the other), and neutral monism (there is one thing that is neither physical nor mental and that one "neutral" thing gives rise to both physical and mental things/properties). We will review each of these in more detail, starting with the most popular: materialism.

Option #1 Materialism:

During the pre-scientific period in the west the influence of spirits was thought to be ubiquitous. Both common and educated people thought that nature was constantly being acted upon by supernatural forces. God and the devil, angels and demons, caused the daily weather, caused eclipses, caused diseases to spread, caused mental illness, and war between nations. They were also cited as the cause of peace between nations, good weather and harvest, and physical and psychological health. These Christian spirits, and the pagan spirits that came before them, were attributed to be the cause of worldly things. Before we had science, all was explained with spirit. This "spirit first" thinking was the prevailing world view. Naturally, this stifled the development of science and technology; the right questions were not being asked. Medieval Europeans often looked for spiritual answers to physical problems. For example, when ravaged by infectious disease they focused narrowly on their societies' moral transgressions that might have awakened the wrath of God. If these medieval thinkers would have focused on potential physical causes, then they might have noticed a connection between their abysmal sanitation practices and the spread of infection. Thus a terrible price was often paid by our pre scientific ancestors for their narrow focus on spiritual rather than physical causation. World views can have real consequences.

Things began to change in the early 17th century. The influential dualistic philosophy of Rene Descartes conceptually separated mind from matter, the spiritual world from the material world. This separation allowed the church to retain its absolute authority in the realm of the spirit and the mind while relinquishing authority over the workings of the physical world to science. This philosophical development, along with the great discoveries of Galileo, Newton, and Copernicus, gave birth to the scientific revolution in which purely physical causes (rather than spiritual) for physical phenomenon were sought and discovered. This search for physical causes of physical phenomenon has been remarkably successful and is borne witness by humanity's tremendous advances in science, medicine, and technology. Therefore, it is not inappropriate to broadly characterize science as the search for physical causes of physical things.

The success of this 400 year old project has prompted most contemporary scientists and philosophers, at least the ones who talk about it, to claim adherence to the metaphysical position of materialism, or what is now sometimes referred to as physicalism[1]. Simply put, materialism means "all is physical", or that there is no reality outside of physical reality. The interactions of matter and energy throughout space and time are the causes for everything in existence. Indeed these are the only things that actually exist. In materialism there is no room for gods and spirits to intervene in the great causal chain of the physical universe. Every phenomenon has a natural and material cause that can ultimately be reduced to the laws of physics.

In today's world this seems to be an obvious conclusion, something so uncontroversial that it hardly needs to be explicitly stated. Stormy weather is not caused by God's wrath, but by the thermodynamic conditions of the atmosphere, which can be described by the laws of physics.

---

[1] *Materialism* is the doctrine that reality is comprised of material substance while the term *physicalism* means more narrowly that reality can be described by the laws of physics. For the most part these two terms can be used interchangeably. However the term materialism will be used in this book due to the fact that all the laws of physics have yet to be discovered. Therefore, because physics is yet to be completely defined, saying that reality can be encompassed by the laws of physics is an unfalsifiable position.

In this limited sense materialism is obviously true. No scientifically minded person could disagree. The questions, however, become more difficult when the focus is turned from physical phenomenon to human beings. What is the human mind in materialism? What is consciousness? Is experience itself a physical process? Adherents to materialism would say yes. In 1949 the British philosopher Gilbert Ryle published his seminal work, *The Concept of Mind,* which boldly confronted the issue. Ryle contested the dualism of Descartes and argued that there was no nonphysical substance in human brains, that there was no, as he puts it, "ghost in the machine". Instead he contended that all that existed was the biochemical machinery of the brain. He argued that no soul, no spirit, no consciousness was needed to explain behavior. All could be explained from a third person perspective. This view was consistent with the psychological school of behaviorism, a popular movement at the time that denied mental constructs as suitable subjects for science and instead tried to recast psychology as the study of observable behavior.

In the late 1950's the analytical behaviorism of Ryle was followed up and surpassed with the birth of "identity theory". Based upon the pioneering writings of Herbert Feigl (1958), J.J.C. Smart (1959), and U.T. Place (1956), identity theory holds that mental processes are physical processes. So that if a feeling of pain is associated with a particular type of brain activity, and they are always linked together, then that experience and the physiological activity can be considered one and the same. In other words, it was argued that states of consciousness are identical, on an ontological level, with the physiological states that produce them. Consciousness can be reduced in its entirety to physical processes in the brain. Nonphysical entities do not exist; therefore absolutely everything in existence is physical, has a physical cause, and can be understood completely by the laws of physics.

Materialism is the dominant position in the modern philosophy of mind. Contemporary articulations of this view fight aggressively against any notion of dualism (e.g., Flanagan, 2003; Levine, 2001; Papineau, 2002). Some versions (e.g., eliminative materialism) refute the idea that there is anything that needs to be explained about consciousness over and above explaining its functions, such as the ability to categorize stimuli or make verbal reports (e.g., Churchland & Churchland, 1998; Dennett, 1991; Rey, 1995). Other versions admit that explaining how experiences arise from neural processing is something that science does not have a good understanding of now, but that there is no reason to conclude that we will not have this understanding sometime in the future (e.g., Dehaene, 2014; Searle, 1997). Still other materialist accounts, while holding on strongly to the belief that conscious experience must be reducible in its entirety to neural functioning, claim that limits in our understanding may keep the process forever out of our reach (McGinn, 1989).

In truth, materialism is a strong logical position to take. Its strength stems primarily from its metaphysical austerity, its parsimony. In other words, because it asserts that only one type of thing exists (physical things) it does not fall into embarrassing paradoxes. It does not have to explain how the ghost (i.e., consciousness) interacts with the machine, because in materialism there is no ghost, only machine. However, parsimony is not all that is important here. Theories are also judged on how much they can explain, and a good ontological theory has to encompass literally everything. What good is a parsimonious theory that has limited explanatory power? This is the point that many arguments against materialism will make, that it is just not up to the task of explaining everything.

Arguments Against Materialism

There are two possible directions that arguments against materialism can take. The first and most common argument is that the motion of molecular particles in the brain is an insufficient explanation or cause of human consciousness. If the being of consciousness cannot be reduced in its entirety to physical processes (matter in motion), then there exists something in the world that is nonphysical. If nonphysical things exist, then the notion that "everything is physical" is not correct and therefore materialism is false.

The second possible direction in which one can argue against materialism centers on the idea that the physical universe does not, and cannot, exist independently of consciousness. This more all-encompassing attack is seldom made by contemporary philosophers. My take on this position will be presented in later chapters throughout this book. However, in what immediately follows I will review three well-established contemporary arguments that attempt to demonstrate that consciousness cannot be reduced to physical processes. These are the *explanatory argument* (Chalmers, 1996; 2010), the *knowledge argument* (Jackson, 1982), and the *conceivability argument* (Chalmers, 1996).

The Explanatory Argument

The term *explanatory gap* was coined in 1983 by the philosopher Joseph Levine. It was meant to describe the inherent difficulty in trying to use physical processes to explain conscious experience. For example, if a neuroscientist discovers that pain is the firing of x set of neurofibers in y region of the brain, although it may be true in a physiological sense, it does not explain how the experience of pain could come from those firings. How could those molecules in motion "be" a burning sensation, how could they "be" any sort of pain or any sort of sensation? Levine holds that even though this explanatory gap currently seems uncloseable, consciousness may still be physical all the same. Levine contends that just because there appears to be a deep epistemic gap that does not necessarily mean that there is an ontological gap[2]. In other words, just because we do not know how matter becomes conscious that does not mean that it is not true; in and of itself the explanatory gap does not prove that consciousness is not physical.

Levine's assertion has been hotly contested by the philosopher David Chalmers (1996, 2010) who argues that the existence of this explanatory gap points to a real divide in nature. He famously refers to the explanatory gap as the "hard problem" of consciousness, the seemingly impossible task of articulating a way in which physical processes

[2] Epistemology is the branch of philosophy concerned with the study of knowledge, and ontology is the branch of philosophy concerned with the study of being, existence. Therefore, an epistemic gap refers to our lack of knowledge about the connection between two things (in this case consciousness and matter) while an ontological gap refers to the idea that there is an actual objective difference between the two things.

might be able to become in themselves conscious experience.

When addressing the explanatory gap, materialists often use examples from settled science to demonstrate the inherent danger in generating ontological conclusions from epistemic premises. They may start with an example of a well-known equivalence, such as that between H_2O and water. They point out that all the facts about the water we observe on a macro physical level can be explained by the facts about the molecule H_2O, why it is a liquid at certain temperatures but not others, why it mixes with salt but not with oil, etc. In this way the macro physical properties of water are said to "emerge" from the microphysical properties of H_2O. Even though it would have been impossible for, let's say, an ancient Roman to understand this emergence, in principle there is no problem. Materialists often contend that this is analogous to consciousness and the physical brain. They argue that all of the facts about consciousness are in principle deducible from the physical facts of neural processing. It is just that we have not sufficiently developed our understanding of the neuroscience of consciousness to deduce them. Therefore, we would be foolish to give up on materialism just because of a limit in our current understanding. In making their case this way, by asserting a type of promissory materialism, they can maintain their *a priori* commitments to a physical cause of consciousness and simultaneously avoid being stymied by the explanatory gap. It is a great strategy for argument as it seems to provide the best of both worlds. However, it is a dodge that appears to fall apart under close examination.

Chalmers (2010) points out that this equivalence between H_2O and water, along with similar equivalences (e.g.,

What are the Constituents of Reality?

DNA and heredity, cellular functioning and life), is an inadequate comparison to the relation between consciousness and the mechanics of neural processing. He argues that the microphysical facts of H_2O are facts only about the structure and dynamics of water molecules, such as how these molecules interact with each other at different temperatures or how they respond to other molecular compounds. While it is absolutely true that this lower level microphysical structure and dynamics explains everything about the higher level macro physical structure and dynamics (e.g., why ice is hard, water is wet, and why water and oil do not mix). It still explains only structure and dynamics. This is what the physical sciences do best, discover facts about lower level (microphysical) structure and dynamics and use them to explain the cause of higher level (macro physical) structure and dynamics. The problem with these analogies is that consciousness is not structure and dynamics. It is qualitative experience, a being of a fundamentally different nature. The feeling of stomach pain, the taste of sugar, and the redness of red are not simply higher level structure and dynamics. Therefore, unlike the wetness of water or the hardness of ice, the emergence of consciousness cannot in principle be explained by lower level structure and dynamics. This is why consciousness resists an explanation in purely physical terms. It is not that we are as ignorant of the mechanism as an ancient Roman would be with molecular chemistry. It is that intrinsic differences between the two domains prohibit the possibility of deriving one from another. It is just as impossible as trying to draw the smell of coffee or play the color green on the piano. Drawings are not smells, notes are not colors, and conscious experience is not physical

11

structure and dynamics. This is the essence of Chalmers' explanatory argument against materialism. It seems to be the simplest argument for the fundamentality of consciousness in the contemporary literature but also the most profound.

The Knowledge Argument

The knowledge argument is a thought experiment described by Frank Jackson (1982, 1986), although the roots of it can be traced to the work of C.D. Broad (1925). Imagine a future neuroscientist named "Mary" who knows absolutely everything about the neurological processes having to do with color vision. She has the total knowledge of an ideal and completed neuroscience. However, she has spent her entire life in a black and white room and has never once had the experience of seeing red. Despite the fact that she has perfect physical knowledge of how color is interpreted in the brain, it seems that she will learn something new when she is allowed to leave the room and see red for the first time. If this is true and Mary gains new knowledge from having the conscious experience of red, then there is more to the experience of red than can be ascertained from perfect knowledge of the molecules in motion in the brain. In other words, it suggests that there are truths about consciousness that are not deducible from physical truths. Even if one knows all of the physical truths there are still experiential truths that are not contained within the physical truths. Therefore, consciousness cannot be solely physical, and materialism is false.

Materialists have attacked this thought experiment in three general ways. The first way is to suggest that Mary does not really learn anything new by seeing red; all she does is gain new knowledge about an old fact (Loar, 1990). The second way is to suggest that by seeing red Mary gains at best a new skill, such as the ability to categorize color (e.g., Lewis, 1983; Nemirow, 2007). Finally using the old standby argument of promissory materialism materialists have argued that a complete resolution to the hard problem will make this all go away. We just cannot understand this yet because the hard problem remains.

While I think that consciousness is fundamental, I do not have a strong opinion as to the intrinsic power of the knowledge argument. I am not sure what it proves or if it is possible to actually prove much from this sort of thought experiment. Looking at it through a logical lens the arguments made against it may very well be correct. However, when one considers it and understands that Mary would have to learn "something new", as I do, it seems that this is based on the intuition that consciousness is not physical, that experience cannot be in itself matter in motion, rather than on the technical form of the argument. In this sense it appears to be an extension of the consequences of the explanatory argument, just presented more colorfully. Still it is a vivid and clever example of the irreducibility of consciousness. It is well worth knowing and studying further. Incidentally, Frank Jackson, the originator of the argument has since changed his mind. After providing dualism with one of its seminal arguments, he now thinks that materialism is the correct metaphysical position (Jackson, 2011).

The Conceivability Argument

The conceivability argument is a more difficult argument

than either the explanatory argument or the knowledge argument. As fully developed by David Chalmers (1996), it starts by asserting that there is no physical reason for consciousness to exist. It is not needed to explain anything about human thoughts, emotions, or behavior. Ironically, this is a point that is shared with many materialists, especially those espousing eliminative materialism (e.g., Dennett, Ryle). From this standpoint, the reason that consciousness exists in the first place is the real mystery. Before we get into the actual argument let me first explain this point further.

It is possible to produce an explanation for every human behavioral action without resorting to consciousness. It can all be done using only matter in motion. For example, consider a person who begins to cry after hearing sad news. The news itself can be reduced to matter in motion (sound waves moving through the molecules that comprise the air). When these waves reach the human ear they are converted into electrical patterns of matter in motion in the ear and brain. These patterns of matter in motion interface with the encoded patterns of matter in motion in the person's memory. This pattern interface is actively processed and subsequently classified as sad news, which is again manifested by a pattern of matter in motion in the prefrontal cortex and limbic areas (charged particles hopping along nerve cells and triggering the release of other particles called neurotransmitters which in turn cause other charged particles to hop along the bodies of different nerve cells). This matter in motion triggers a further patterned chain of matter in motion that affects the person's tear ducts and breathing producing the phenomena that we call crying. If other people are watching and listening to this scene, matter in motion as described earlier activates the mirror neurons (neurons that help us process other people's perspectives) in the onlookers, which by a similar physiological process results in behaviors associated with the concept of empathy (e.g., worried facial expressions, verbal expressions of concern, etc.).

Thus a very emotional scene involving behaviors associated with sadness and empathy, perhaps even anxiety in some of the onlookers, does not require these feelings to occur. It requires no consciousness. In fact science has yet to identify a single physical reason for consciousness to exist. The complex behavior described in the preceding scene could be accomplished by what Chalmers calls zombies, beings that act as though they are conscious but exist without qualia, without internal experience. Their brains, unlike ours, simply do not produce consciousness. Now of course zombies do not actually exist (as far as we know). But that is not the issue. What is important is whether or not we can conceive of them existing.

The conceivability argument can be simply stated as such. It is conceivable for brains to exist that do not produce consciousness (we just conceived of it two paragraphs ago). By "conceivable" Chalmers means logically coherent; for example a circle of elephants a hundred miles in diameter is conceivable, but a circle that contains an angle is not conceivable. Using the standard methodology of analytical philosophy something is metaphysically possible if and only if it is first conceivable, and something that is conceivable (while maybe not likely) will nevertheless remain a metaphysical possibility. Therefore, Chalmers argues that because it is conceivable then it is also metaphysically possible for nonconscious brains to exist. However, since materialism requires that our consciousness experiences actually "be" matter in motion, to believe in materialism means that you must hold that zombies are metaphysically impossible, that they are inconceivable. In other words, if consciousness is entirely physical it should be absolutely "necessary" that conscious experience always co-occur with its physical correlate, because, according to materialism, it is ontologically isomorphic to that physical correlate. It should be impossible to consider them apart from each other in a logically coherent way. Thinking about it as two separate things should be as hard to do as thinking about a square without right angles, or an odd number that is divisible by two. Since it is possible to consider one without the other, then according to Chalmers, they are ontologically distinct, which means that all is not physical and therefore materialism is false.

The conceivability argument can get complicated. It is thick with philosophical assumptions about the rules of reasoning itself and remains a subject of ongoing debate within the philosophy of mind literature. My primary motivation for presenting it here was to make the vital point that there is no known physical or logical reason that consciousness should accompany the patterns of matter in motion in human brains. It is not needed to explain anything about how we behave or about how the brain works. From a purely physical perspective, the phenomenon of consciousness exists without being necessitated.

In addition to the three I presented, there are several other widely known arguments against materialism in contemporary philosophy that were not included in the forgoing: Thomas Nagel's (1974) *what it is like to be a bat argument*, Saul Kripke's (1981) *modal argument for dualism*, and the *argument from revelation* (Johnston, 1997). Interested readers may want to explore these further. Some of these arguments may turn out to be valid while others may not. For my money a careful consideration of the explanatory argument is all that I believe is necessary. I have a deep sense, one that I cannot yet articulate, that all of the others may just be increasingly more clever ways of demonstrating that consciousness is something that is fundamentally different than higher level structure and dynamics.

Option # 2 Dualism

If you believe that the universe is comprised of independently existing objective matter and space, but are sympathetic to the idea that such matter in motion could not possibly "be" experience, then you are a dualist. As the name would suggest, dualism splits reality into two ontologically equal components of mind and matter, or physical and nonphysical. In dualism consciousness and physical reality are both fundamental. Neither one is derived from the other.

The prevalence of dualistic thought in philosophy and the sciences lags far behind that of materialism. Dualists are a distinct minority. Many materialists consider it to be an immature position, an old fashioned way of reasoning that has not evolved enough to dispel the religious concept of the soul from the actual physical reality of science. Despite this, articulations of dualist thought can be found across a variety of disciplines such as physics (Stapp, 2003;

17

2005; Walker, 1998), philosophy (Chalmers, 2010; Nagel, 1974), neurophysiology (Beck & Eccles, 1998), and even psychiatry (Swartz et al, 2002).

There are problems with dualism though. To be clear, I am in full agreement with the dualists that consciousness is fundamental (that it cannot be derived from physical processes). However, by simultaneously maintaining that matter is fundamental they get themselves into tight spots. I believe that this is where they error. Why should the universe be split into two independent ontological regions? If you examine most materialist arguments against dualism in the philosophy of mind literature you will find that the arguments are usually not formed to directly attack the fundamentality of conscious experience, but rather the attack is levied on the problem of explaining how nonphysical consciousness and objectively existing physical matter could ever interact. Thus the arguments are directed against the idea that the universe is bifurcated into two separate domains. If consciousness is nonphysical how can it have any effect on the physical workings of the brain, and how, if consciousness were really nonphysical, would neural activity be able to have any effect on the content of a person's conscious experiences? There is simply no bridge between the two. Typically, after expounding on this physical to nonphysical interaction problem they quickly assert (rightly so) that this problem disappears if we simply assume that the world is comprised of only one thing. Since, in their eyes, idealism is implicitly considered an untenable position, the only rational option left is materialism. Any problem with explaining how a physical process can create experience is met with the seemingly reasonable assertion that it just has to. There is nothing else from which it could arise. It is far better to have an intractable explanatory problem than to resort to thinking that our physical brains are possessed by immortal spirits. Materialism is thereby cast as the only modern and serious solution.

I think that this is an excellent argument strategy. It forces dualists into a corner and seeks to make their position look like a weak appeal to the concept of the soul. The problem, however, is that materialists completely ignore the inverse question: why are we so sure that matter is fundamental? This is never explained. It is just assumed to be true at the onset. Now this would not be such a problem if we did not have such strong arguments that consciousness is fundamental. But since there are good independent reasons to think that consciousness is fundamental, and dualism appears to suffer from an inability to explain the interaction problem, then we should at least consider the possibility that matter may not be as fundamental as it seems. Intellectual honesty should force us to seriously explore our third option: idealism.

Option # 3 Idealism:

Idealism[3] is the position that all is consciousness, or that all is able to be reduced to consciousness. Idealists do not

---

[3] There are different types of idealism that warrant clarification. First there is a distinction between objective and subjective idealism. Objective idealism is the idealism of Plato, who argued that objects in the world are mere shadows of an ideal objects in the ideal realm of the forms. In contrast, subjective idealism is the theory that conscious experience is the primary constituent of reality. There is also the distinction between epistemic and metaphysical idealism, where epistemic idealism refers to the relative nature of knowledge, the lack of an objective truth, and metaphysical idealism pertains to consciousness's role in the nature of reality. When I say idealism, I am referring to subjective and metaphysical idealism.

have to find a way for matter to create consciousness, just as materialists do not have to find a way for consciousness to create matter. In idealism consciousness is a given. It is the ground of all that is, just as in materialism, matter (i.e., physical reality) is a given. The "hard problem" in idealism is to explain how consciousness creates matter, or more accurately the phenomenological experience of matter. It is the exact opposite of the hard problem within materialism. My view, which will be presented in latter chapters throughout this book, is that unlike the hard problem of materialism the hard problem of idealism has a readymade solution.

Idealism solves the dualist's dilemma of how consciousness and an objectively existing physical reality could ever interact by denying the objective presence of physical reality. In idealism, what we consider to be physical reality is not independent of consciousness. It is made for consciousness. It is dependent on it. Therefore, because it asserts that only one type of thing (consciousness) exists, idealism is every bit as parsimonious as materialism.

Idealism has a long and storied history going back thousands of years. In the east we find its earliest expression in the Purusha Sukta, a pantheistic Hindu text of the Rig Veda (1500–1200 B.C.E.) where the cosmic being Purusha is seen as pervading the entire universe. Idealist notions continue on through classical Hindu philosophy and are prominent in both the Vedanta and Yoga schools of thought. However, these idealistic philosophies are closely tied with the Hindu's deities and therefore appear to be inseparable from the Hindu religion.

In the west idealism had its first articulation in the speculations of the Greek philosopher Anaxagoras (500

B.C.E.). He proposed that mind was the organizing principle that brought the chaos of the early universe into order. He thought that in the beginning of time all physical things were one, that the elements were not yet separated from each other. Hot and cold, light and darkness, moist and dry, were all intermingled and not yet disentangled into the separateness and the order that we now observe. He reasoned that the being that separated these physical constituents could not itself be physical or it would get drawn into this intermingling and could not act to direct it. He therefore postulated "mind" as the force that achieved this saying, "All things were together: then mind came and gave them order". This mind can be thought of as being religious in nature, a detached god like mind. This view may have eventually got him into trouble with the state sponsored mythologies of his time. He is said to have been indicted in Athens on the charge of promoting doctrines subversive of religion.

In the early modern period in the west a collection of idealistic ontologies were presented by philosophers such as George Berkeley (1685-1753), Johann Fichte (1762–1814), Friedrich Schelling (1775–1854), Georg Hegel (1770–1831), and Arthur Schopenhauer (1788-1860). Like the idealisms that had come before them these philosophies were generally of a religious nature. Although they represented significant advances in thought, the concept of the Christian God often was a necessary component, an underwriter of the metaphysics. For example, Berkeley writes of God that, "He alone it is who upholding all things by the word of his power maintains that intercourse between spirits, whereby they are able to perceive the existence of each other".

Idealistic thought continued into the turn of last century. Without dependence on religious concepts, the British philosopher F. H. Bradley (1893) argued that existence required sentient experience, that physical reality could not exist independently of consciousness. He writes:

> "We perceive, on reflection, that to be real, or even barely to exist, must be to fall within sentience..... Find any piece of existence, take up anything that anyone could possibly call a fact, or could in any sense assert to have being, and then judge if it does not consist in sentient experience. Try to discover any sense in which you can still continue to speak of it, when all perception and feeling have been removed; or point out any fragment of its matter, any aspect of its being, which is not derived from and is not still relative to this source. When the experiment is made strictly, I can myself conceive of nothing else than the experienced."

> *-Appearance and Reality*

By the early 20th century, rather than being the sole purview of philosophy, idealism starts to be pushed by certain scientists. For example, the physicist James Jeans (1930) contends:

> "The stream of knowledge is heading towards a non-mechanical reality; the Universe begins to look more like a great thought than like a great machine. Mind no longer appears to be an accidental intruder into the realm of matter... we ought

rather hail it as the creator and governor of the realm of matter."

-The Mysterious Universe

In contemporary times the case has been made by scientists such as Bernard d'Espagnat, (1979), Robert Lanza (2009), and Amit Goswami (1990) that advances in our understanding of microphysical reality (i.e., quantum mechanics) have destroyed the possibility of conceptualizing matter as having an objective presence independent of consciousness. Lastly, the cognitive scientist Donald Hoffman (2007) makes the argument that idealism makes sense from an evolutionary perspective. He contends that reality is comprised of conscious agents whose interactions can be mathematically modeled without reliance on the concept of an objective physical reality.

Option # 4 Neutral Monism:

In recent years that idea of neutral monism has gained some popularity. Instead of assuming that reality is broken into two separate domains (dualism) or that it is monistic in that it is either all consciousness or all physical, neutral monism holds that there is one thing, a neutral substance out of which both mind and matter, the physical and the nonphysical, arise. This view appears to have been first expounded by the Dutch philosopher Baruch Spinoza (1632-1677). It was subsequently championed in the early 20th century by the psychologist William James (1912) and the philosopher Bertrand Russell (1921).

The problem with neutral monism is that we do not have a good sense of what this neutral substance could be or how it could work to produce our observable reality. It has been suggested that elementary particles of matter may hold on to protophenomenological qualities that, when organized in a brain, manifest themselves as complex experience. While this approach certainly has promise, its adherents have yet to take the first step, which would be to demonstrate how it would be possible to have, let's say, conscious electrons. Therefore, due to its underdevelopment, I do not see it as a viable metaphysical framework at this time. However it remains a possibility and deserved to be mentioned in this brief survey.

Summary of the Four Metaphysical Options

Metaphysical Options:	The Nature of Physical Substance:	The Nature of Consciousness:
Materialism	Fundamental	Derived from physical substance
Dualism	Fundamental	Fundamental
Idealism	Derived from Consciousness	Fundamental
Neutral Monism	Derived from a neutral substance	Derived from a neutral substance

Religion and the Road Ahead

As I stated at the beginning of this chapter, my goal is to convince you that the primary constituent of reality is consciousness, that idealism is the correct metaphysical option. However, unlike the vast majority of idealistic philosophies throughout history, the present work aims to articulate an idealism that is all together separate from religion. As indicated in the title of this book, it will be a naturalistic idealism. No level of belief will be required. The point of this separation is simple. There is only one reality, and there are many religions. By attaching an ontological framework to a particular religious orientation, by mixing together philosophical/scientific and religious concepts, one is bound to create a philosophy that is simultaneously rejected by the majority of readers from every other religious orientation along with all of the atheists. Staying free of these concepts is the only way to give the ideas that will be presented here a fighting chance. Therefore the concepts will not be mixed and the following will aim to be a wholly secular endeavor. Having said that, I also want to add that this separation in concepts should not be interpreted as antipathy towards religion. There are aspects of both eastern and western religious traditions that may fit nicely within the framework (although everything could also be understood in a secular way as well). I will leave it to the reader to contemplate these issues further within their own perspectives.

2

Doubting the Objective Presence of Matter

"As a man who has devoted his whole life to the most clear headed science, to the study of matter, I can tell you as a result of my research about atoms this much: There is no matter as such. All matter originates and exists only by virtue of a force which brings the particle of an atom to vibration and holds this most minute solar system of the atom together. We must assume behind this force the existence of a conscious and intelligent Mind. This Mind is the matrix of all matter."

— Max Planck, *Das Wesen der Materie*, 1944
Nobel Laureate

"What is real.…..If real is what you can feel, smell, taste and see, then 'real' is simply electrical signals interpreted by your brain."

—Morpheus, *The Matrix*, 1999

The vast majority of contemporary scientists and philosophers would classify themselves as adherents to materialism, whereas a lesser number would consider themselves to be dualists or adherents to neutral monism. However, it is indubitable that the least popular of the metaphysical frameworks is idealism. Materialism, dualism, and neutral monism all differ as to the extent in which they consider consciousness as fundamental, but they all start with the

assumption that the physical world is in some way fundamental. In none of these three most common metaphysical frameworks is the independent existence of physical reality ever questioned, let alone rigorously scrutinized as it
should be. In the modern age, the existence of an independent physical reality is just assumed, without proof, to
be an obvious fact. I believe this assumption is an error.
There is no reason for such confidence. In the 21st century
we appear to have long forgotten that for hundreds of
years philosophers have wrestled with the fact that there
appears to be no way to prove the existence of an independent physical reality outside of consciousness. Reac-
quainting ourselves with their work will provide the necessary perspective to critically evaluate the assumed
ontological superiority of the physical over the nonphysical.

Systematic Rational Doubt

The French philosopher Rene Descartes (1596-1650) was
the most famous doubter in the history of western thought.
At the dawn of the early modern period he set out to develop a method that would unify reason. Descartes asserted that there existed in each person an innate human
reasoning ability that can lead to truth. Disagreements on
what the truth is lay not in some people possessing more
or less reasoning capability than others, but that people
started reasoning from different points. Therefore, he
thought that if he could clear the ground of erroneous beliefs he could build a temple of universal reason that eve-
ryone could summit and thereby arrive at the same conclusions.

In order to build on the firmest foundation, Descartes determined that he must first clear his mind of any belief of which he was not absolutely certain, of any idea that he could doubt in the slightest. To keep himself honest and his pursuit pure he decided that he would assume to be false any idea that was not beyond doubt. First, Descartes attacked the data from his own senses (i.e., what he saw, what he heard). He reasoned that since his senses have deceived him in the past they are subject to doubt. Therefore, applying his method, any information obtained through his senses could not be wholly trusted to be true and should be assumed to be false. He then extends this reasoning and considers occasions when he is in a dream and he thought that he was seeing, feeling, and tasting things, only to wake up and find that all of his perceptions of action were false and that he was lying quietly in his bed the whole time. Since in his dreams he has even dreamt that he was someone else, he then has reason to doubt the existence of his sense organs themselves and indeed the nature of his entire body.

Taking his doubt further still, Descartes considers matters of logical and mathematical necessity, such as the idea that $2 + 2 = 4$. Certainly this level of truth is beyond the doubt that could be applied to his senses. Should not $2 + 2 = 4$ in a dream as well as in reality? However, Descartes recognized that he has made mistakes in logical and mathematical reasoning before, being absolutely sure of the truth of a proposition only to later realize that his reasoning was not as unassailable as he had previously thought. Therefore, according to his method, he must assume false every analytical conclusion he has ever made.

In a final crescendo of doubt, Descartes assumes that

he has no body and exists as nothing more than a brain in a vat of liquid. He imagines that he is kept alive this way by an evil demon who is controlling all of his perceptions and is making him think that he is a man with a body living in the outside world. What he believes to be his body is not really his body, and the objects that he perceives through his senses are not caused by actual objects but are deceptive manipulations. Under this nightmare scenario every bit of information that Descartes could gain about the outside world would be false. Since this scenario cannot be ruled out, Descartes concludes that just about everything he has ever thought becomes subject to doubt and is assumed to be false.

At this point Descartes appears to have dug himself into a hole from which there is no escape. The obtainment of any unquestionable knowledge seems to be impossible. It is at this lowest moment when epiphany strikes, an epiphany that will give him what he believed to be his first piece of unassailable knowledge. Descartes realized that he could not doubt that he was experiencing doubt; he could not doubt that he was conscious of his own experience at the time that it was occurring. That experience could be true or false, it could be an accurate representation of external reality or it could be the work of a deceptive sense organ, the result of a dream or the product of an evil demon, however it could not be doubted that such an experience existed. Even the all-powerful evil demon could not make him doubt that he was experiencing what he was experiencing. This brings Descartes to declare that experience (consciousness) is fundamental. This is the origin of the famous "Cogito ergo sum": I think therefore I am. Descartes writes:

> "I thence concluded that I was a substance whose whole essence or nature consists only in thinking, and which, that it may exist, has need of no place, nor is dependent on any material thing"

— Discourse on the Method

The philosophy of Descartes gave rise to a profound dualism between mind and matter. This is his legacy. It is almost impossible to escape the influence of this dualism today as it laid the very foundation for the growth of science in the centuries following his death. However Cartesian doubt need not lead directly to dualism. It can be interpreted in other ways. In my view Descartes' doubt simply highlighted the ontological separation between mind (consciousness) and matter. For Descartes, the existence of his conscious experience was beyond doubt, while the existence of everything physical had to be taken on faith. This is the first necessary step toward idealism, although Descartes chose to travel no further.

Those readers who have seen the 1999 film, "The Matrix" will recognize Descartes' theme of an evil demon. The story is set in a future world where computers dominate humankind and have implanted a false sensory reality into their brains; whereas they think they are free when they are really enslaved, they think that they are walking and talking when they are really entombed in energy sucking pods, and they think that they are living at the end of the twentieth century, when they are really living hundreds of years in the future. The film, which of course is based on Descartes' 400 year old ideas, has invigorated philosophical discussion regarding the possibility of simulated realities. For example, the philosopher Nickolas Bostrom (2003) argues that not only would we have no way to prove that what we currently believe to be reality is not simulated, but that it is possible that we are almost certainly living in a simulation right now. The argument proceeds like this. One of the following scenarios must be true. (1) Either the intelligent beings that inhabit the universe never develop the technological sophistication needed to produce simulated realities, (2) or they do but create very few of them, (3) or they do and create many of them. If the third scenario is correct, then odds are we are almost certainly living inside a simulation. Since there is only one reality if there are many simulations the chances are overwhelming that what you believe to be reality is merely one of those many simulations. The possibilities are boundless. Our creators could care deeply about us, much in the same way that the great religions contend that we are watched over by a loving god. It is also possible that our creators do not know that we are conscious and hence do not care about our feelings or suffering. Maybe our world is being simulated to investigate possible solutions to some social or technological problem in the world of our creators. Or maybe our creator is a futuristic sadist who knows that we are conscious and, because he enjoys watching us suffer, sets the preconditions for wars, disease, and natural disasters. All of these scenarios are possible. None of them can be absolutely ruled out.

The speculations of Descartes and contemporary philosophers such as Bostrom remind us that there are limits to what we can be certain of outside of our own conscious experience. It must be accepted that any knowledge obtained about the outside world, or even its very existence, is and must always be, predicated on assumptions that can never be verified. Therefore, there is, and always will be, room for doubt.

A Radically Empirical Approach

George Berkley (1685-1753), an Irish philosopher born nearly a century after Descartes, takes his doubt to the next level and denies the existence of mind independent objects. He called his philosophical position "immaterialism" and contented that the reality of objects is maintained not in the things themselves, but in them being perceived. Berkeley reasoned that the sense impressions that an object makes on an observer (e.g., color, shape, sound, smell etc.) are the first order data and that the corporeal presence of the object itself is superfluous. In other words, he contends that the concept of matter is an ontological extravagance that is not necessary to explain sense data. The most parsimonious approach, Berkeley reasons, is to assume that sense data in itself is the ultimate constituent of reality and that objects themselves are an unnecessary appendage, a speculation. Berkeley's conclusions may sound absurd at first. However, upon reflection, you may recognize it for what it is: a simplistic empirical approach.

It may help to relate this to Descartes' reasoning. Implicit in Descartes' thought is the idea that there is an "outside world" independent of the conscious observer. Descartes, due to his faith in the existence of a god that would not deceive him, assumes at the onset that there is such a thing as a mind independent physical world. Therefore, he never doubts the existence of this world, only what could be known about it. His philosophy then, even after demonstrating the ontological separation between mind and matter, remains focused on what could be known about this outside reality that he assumes to exist due to faith. For him there is a separation between knowledge and reality, between epistemology and ontology.

In contrast, Berkeley, in a radically empirical move, chooses to accept the sense impressions of consciousness as the first order data of which reality is comprised. He was not concerned with whether sense data was a true or false reflection of some outside physical reality. For Berkeley, the question of whether a particular sense impression is true or false is completely meaningless. All sense impressions are true. They are true because they are being experienced. They cannot be doubted because, for him, there existed no outside reality for the sense data to be incongruent with. Thus Berkeley solves the age old problem of appearance and reality by asking why must there be a reality outside of appearance. If all we can experience is sense data, then there is no reason not to assume that this is all there is. For Berkeley appearance is reality: to be is to be perceived. Shortly into his master work, *A Treatise Concerning the Principles of Human Knowledge*, he writes the following:

> "It is indeed an opinion strangely prevailing amongst men, that houses, mountains, rivers, and in a word all sensible objects have an existence natural or real, distinct from their being perceived by the understanding. But with how great an assurance and acquiescence soever this principle may be entertained in the world; yet whoever shall find in his heart to call it in question, may, if I mistake not, perceive it to involve a manifest

contradiction. For what are the forementioned objects but the things we perceive by sense, and what do we perceive besides our own ideas or sensations; and is it not plainly repugnant that any one of these or any combination of them should exist unperceived?"

What Berkeley is saying is that we can only perceive "ideas" (by this he means sense data, conscious experience). So that even when in common language we may say that we perceive physical objects, we are actually only perceiving ideas. Therefore, he reasons that objects must be ideas. If not, Berkeley then asks what direct proof do we have that objects are not ideas. He explores whether or not it would be possible to prove the existence of a mind independent material reality by either our sense experiences or our reason (logic). He takes on senses first. He points out (using Descartes' reasoning) that sense data cannot prove the existence of anything but sense data. He then concludes that a mind independent material reality, if it were to exist, would need to be proven to exist by reason. Again following Descartes' line of reasoning he contends that there is no reason to infer this because of what occurs during dreams and other such scenarios clearly demonstrates that conscious experience need not coincide with what one assumes to be an external reality outside of perception.

In addition to the preceding, Berkley gives us his "master argument" for idealism. Simply put, Berkley asks whether it is possible for a thing to exist (let us say a tree) without being perceived. For it to be possible for a thing to exist without being perceived it would first have to be conceivable for it to exist without being perceived. In other words, we would need to be able to imagine a scenario of a tree so isolated from civilization that it is never perceived by any human. Here in lies the problem, it is impossible to conceive of an object existing without being perceived because to conceive of it is to simultaneously perceive it. Berkley implies that our inability to do so is not simply an inconsequential logical paradox but a glimpse into the fundamental nature of reality. The argument is circular for sure, but that seems to be the point. In the mind of a philosopher existence cannot be separated from perception because in reality existence cannot be separated from perception.

Critics have attacked Berkley's system due to its inability to deal with what happens while an object is not being observed. Does it then not exist only to spring back into existence once observed again? This is a problem for Berkley's immaterialism. The answer he provides is that all objects are held in existence by the omnipotence of god, whose mind is constantly observing all of creation. Although acceptable during the age in which he gave it, that answer is insufficient by today's standards, even for philosophers who are themselves religious. This is the central hole in Berkley's thought as he presented it. For immaterialism to be taken seriously today the problem of the existence of objects outside of observation needs to be addressed without resorting to theism.

The philosophies of Descartes and Berkley have set the stage for the modern era, and its questions on the matter. Although most contemporary philosophers believe that a mind independent reality exists, and there are many valid criticisms of the philosophical systems erected by both

Descartes and Berkeley, most of the great philosophers since have acknowledged that the existence of a mind independent reality is not at all obvious, and many have contended that it is likely to be an unprovable proposition. For example, Immanuel Kant (1724-1804), perhaps the greatest philosopher of the 18th century, and himself a harsh critic of Berkley's immaterialism, famously laments:

> "It still remains a scandal to philosophy and to human reason in general that the existence of things outside us must be accepted merely on faith, and that if anyone thinks good to doubt their existence, we are unable to counter his doubts by any satisfactory proof."

> —*Critique of Pure Reason*

In 1921 Bertrand Russell, arguably the most prominent philosopher of the early 20th century agrees with Kant's assessment and states:

> "it must be admitted that we can never prove the existence of things other than ourselves and our experience"

> —*Problems of Philosophy*

However, he adds to it, pointing out that lack of proof of a proposition does not necessarily require us to doubt it.

> "it may be that the whole outer world is nothing but a dream and that we alone exist. This is an uncomfortable possibility; but although it cannot

be strictly proved to be false, there is not the slightest reason to suppose that this is the case."

—*Problems of Philosophy*

Thus Russell asserts that the improvability of the persistence of physical reality outside of observation should not stop us from believing in its existence. Just because a proposition may not be able to be proven, it is not in and of itself a reason to doubt it, being that there is an absence of reason to doubt. While I agree with Russell's logic, I disagree that "there is not the slightest reason to suppose that this is the case". I think that there is ample reason to doubt the existence of an independent physical reality. The following two chapters will be devoted to fully explaining this reason.

3

The Essesential Nature of Matter and Energy

"The ontology of materialism rested upon the illusion that the kind of existence, the direct 'actuality' of the world around us, can be extrapolated into the atomic range. This extrapolation, however, is impossible... atoms are not things."

—Werner Heisenberg
Nobel Laureate

Reality seems to present us with different types of "being". For example, my right foot has being, so does the experience of the headache that I am starting to develop, as does the planet Mars, the Pythagorean Theorem, and Beethoven's 5th Symphony. My headache is a being different from the being of my foot, both of which are different from the mathematical relationship between the sides of a triangle. Even a particular being we named, such as Beethoven's 5th, can have multiple manifestations. When we say Beethoven's 5th do we mean the original musical manuscript, the sound waves moving through the air, the experience of hearing it, or the notes in the abstract? Books have been written on this subject alone and for our purpose it is best not to stray too far off course. Therefore, I want to focus here on a particular type of being whose nature it is to have all of its being contained within its essence (i.e., its defining information). It will henceforth be referred to as *essesential being* for this very reason.

For an example of essesential being consider the concept of the number 3. Its existence is solely and entirely its essence. It 'is' 2 + 1, 5 - 2, the halfway point between 2 and 4, the square root of 9, or any other mathematical expression of its essence. It is a thing which exists as, and only as, its defining information. Existing in this way it can never allow something new to be known about itself. It can never develop further characteristics; it can never grow or become damaged. It cannot change with time because it has within itself no being over time. Therefore, the number 3, as part of its essesential nature, is fundamentally atemporal (i.e., free of time).

Consider also that the number 3 is internally homogenous; it has no differentiable parts. A 3 is made up only of 3. It has no components, no front, no back, no middle, and no sides. Place this in contrast to an object such as an automobile which is internally heterogeneous. It has an engine, a trunk, a steering wheel, four tires, and a windshield. While these parts and others come together to comprise an "automobile", none of these components is in itself an "automobile". The whole is not contained in each part.

A further characteristic of essesential beings, a direct consequence of their internal homogeneity, is that they are indistinguishable from all others of the same type. There is no way to tell one 3 apart from another as they all have the same fundamental properties; they exist only as these fundamental properties. It should be noted that essesential beings could exist in different positions relative to a point of reference, physical or conceptual, and remain indistinguishable. For example, the first 3 in a number such as 333 has a different meaning than the last 3, in that it is in the hundreds place and represents a different value due to that position. However, conceptually speaking, those are indistinguishable 3s; their position relative to each other or some other number does not change the fact that they exist in themselves as, and only as, their essence.

Numbers, symbols, and other abstract human constructs are not the only beings that exist solely as their essence. Remarkably, the elementary particles in the standard model of particle physics, the fundamental constituents of matter and energy in our universe, appear to also be examples of essesential being. This assertion can be made because, like numbers, elementary particles are internally homogeneous and indistinguishable from others of the same type. See the chart on the next page.

Essesential Matter & Energy

The Periodic Table of Elementary Particles and Forces

Three Generations
of Matter (Fermions)

These elementary particles cannot be broken down into smaller scales. The atoms that comprise the matter that we deal with every day are comprised of electrons, which is itself an elementary particle, and protons and neutrons that are comprised of a combination of quarks (a proton is comprised of two up quarks and one down quark, and a neutron is comprised of two down quarks and one up quark.).

In a nontrivial way, these elementary particles exist solely as their essence, as a type of number 3 for the physical world. We define an elementary particle by its mass, charge, and spin, which constitute a description of its essence. All of the elementary particles that comprise the physical universe can be defined and distinguished in such a way based on these measurements. We can ask the question, would it be possible for an elementary particle to exist in a mode beyond its essence, or more operationally put, can it exist in a way that makes it distinguishable from all other elementary particles of the same type? The answer from physics is "no". Every elementary particle, like every number 3, is both theoretically and practically indistinguishable from every other elementary particle of the same type that has ever existed anywhere in the universe. In other words, particles do not have individual characters; they are all exactly the same. Physicists call this the principle of indistinguishability of elementary particles. It is a cornerstone of particle physics and molecular chemistry. It is an empirical fact of science.

However, if elementary particles are essesential, then all that is comprised of them, the matter and energy of the physical universe, must also exist only as its essence. There appears to be no way to escape this conclusion. The complexity of the information held in this essence increases exponentially as one moves from an elementary particle, to subatomic particle, to the buildings in New York City. However, simply increasing the information in something's aggregate essence does not allow the thing to exist beyond it. We could write a number a hundred trillion digits long that would have tremendous complexity, but it could still be described completely in terms of its essence, meaning it would still exist as, and only as, its defining information. In this sense, matter (energy) is like a collection of numbers, abstractions of type, and should be ontologically viewed as such.

This startling consequence of elementary particles' essesential nature is rarely appreciated as it should be. In fact, it has been outright ignored. I suspect that this is due in part to the language that we use to talk about them. The popular metaphor that elementary particles are "building blocks" works to obscure the truth. The problem is that macro physical terms related to construction (i.e., blocks, bricks) do not accurately translate down to the microphysical level. Whereas no two bricks are exactly the same, elementary particles are perfect manifestations of their mathematical ideal. When they are referred to as "building blocks" they are implicitly endowed with the conceptual attributes of distinguishability and internal heterogeneity, traits they simply do not possess. It is an unintentional bait and switch that hides the illogical conclusion that it is possible for matter to be essesential at a micro physical level while holding onto existence beyond its essence at a macro physical level.

Although it currently does not appear to be the majority opinion, this viewpoint, that elementary particles are not described by information but actually are information, has been gaining some traction in physics over the last several decades. Most notably the physicist Max Tegmark (2008, 2014) in his Mathematical Universe Hypothesis contends that the components of physical reality are mathematical objects, meaning that they exist without fundamental intrinsic properties outside of their mathematical properties. He writes, "Whereas the customary terminology in physics

43

textbooks is that external reality is described by mathematics, the Mathematical Universe Hypothesis states that it is mathematics".[4] Other physicists such as John Wheeler (1990) have similarly contended that at its basic level physical reality appears to be based on information itself as opposed to independently persisting objects that are merely described by information. Although I seem to agree on this point with both Tegmark and Wheeler, there are massive differences between us on how we view the origin of this information based reality as well as its consequences. Nevertheless, the view that the world appears to be built from components that are in themselves abstractions does have adherents within physics, or at the very least it is certainly not ruled out in any way.

To reiterate, the elementary particles that comprise the matter and energy of the physical universe appear to be examples of essesential being; like numbers and other abstractions they appear to be able to hold on to no being beyond their essence. This conclusion is a direct consequence of the fact that elementary physical particles are indivisible and homogenous. Interestingly, the idea that the world is comprised of indivisible homogeneous particles is far from new. It actually predates, by millennia, the origin of science itself. The roots of matter's essesential nature were uncovered by the Greeks of antiquity. Amid a complete absence of any technology that could apprehend the problem empirically, they derived the first atomic theories of matter just by thinking about it.

---

[4] Although I agree with Tegmark on this point, he uses the idea that reality may be information based to make an argument for objective realism, the exact opposite of where we are headed here.

Essesential Matter & Energy

A Modern Idea in Ancient Times

In the century before the time of Socrates, Greek thought was characterized by attempts to comprehend reality through a single broad intellectual grasp. The sciences had not yet been separated from each other, and all of science was still undifferentiated from philosophy, which had just begun to separate itself from religion and mythology. From this Greek enlightenment came the foundational ideas of western civilization and consequently science itself. The two great giants of this pre-Socratic period were Heraclitus (480 B.C.E) and Parmenides (500 B.C.E.). Their profoundly different visions of reality created a conceptual tension that the first atomic theory was produced to remedy.

From what has survived we know that Heraclitus thought that the organizing principle of reality was change itself. In his ontology nothing is stable or even able to remain identical with itself. To be is literally to change. For Heraclitus reality is not comprised of being but of becoming. Heraclitus deals with the appearance of things which seem to remain identical with themselves by contending that the appearance of identity is but an illusion. To illustrate his point he provides the example of a river whose water flow is constantly changing, although it gives the appearance of being something permanent.

The complete opposite conclusion of Heraclitus can be found in the thoughts of Parmenides. For him all change was an illusion, a trick of the senses. To even think of nonbeing is impossible. In his ontology there is nothing that exists outside of being. Everything is. Being is one and indivisible having no beginning and no end. There is no such thing as temporal change because past, present, and future are all one. Parmenides arrives at this homogeneous unity of being through the following reasoning. Being must be one because if it were manifold, if it had parts, it would require that there be something to divide the parts. Since nonbeing, by definition, does not exist it could not be used to divide being into parts. If being were used to divide being into parts, then there is no division for all would be being. Therefore all is being, and this being is one.

The philosopher Democritus (460 B.C.E.) inherited the great ontological chasm between Parmenides and Heraclitus. In order to move forward he needed to find a way out of this impasse. His attempt to account for the reality of change, while retaining as much as possible from Parmenides' system, leads him to create the first atomic theory of matter. Democritus' solution is ingenious. He takes Parmenides' being, atemporal and homogenous, and shrinks it into tiny indivisible parts which he calls "atoms" (literally meaning in Greek that which cannot be divided, uncuttable[5]). Apart from these atoms is simply void. By being able to move through this void the continuous motion of atoms gives rise to the constant change observed by Heraclitus. In this system Parmenides' unchangeable indivisible being is saved, only that it is now contained within an infinite number of tiny atoms moving throughout the void.

---

[5] What Democritus is calling atoms we are calling elementary particles. The word atom (meaning uncutable) was used up too soon to name structures that we later learned have parts (i.e., electrons, protons, and neutrons).

The reasoning Democritus uses to arrive at his conclusion was said to go like this.[6] If you divide something an infinite number of times the sections you are left with would have to either have magnitude or not have magnitude. If after an infinite number of divisions the sections contained magnitude, then if you multiply that magnitude (no matter how small) by the infinite number of sections you would be left with the impossible result of an object that is infinitely large. On the other hand, if each section had zero magnitude, then even if you multiplied it by the infinite number of sections you would still have zero magnitude for the whole, another impossible result. Democritus reasoned that since this paradox results from assuming things are infinitely divisible then things must not be infinitely divisible. There must exist a smallest part of things that cannot be further divided. This smallest uncuttable part (the atom) must also be completely homogeneous in nature because if it itself had parts or any other sign of heterogeneity then it would have more than one part and could not be itself the smallest part. Therefore, he concluded that the world must be comprised of internally homogeneous indivisible particles.

Democritus developed his theory fully making many speculations as to the nature of these atoms. He contended that these atoms vary according to shape order and position. They exist in infinite number and in infinite variety. They are homogeneous throughout and lack internal structure. They are in constant motion. For Democritus all of reality can be understood in terms of the local interactions

---

[6] What we know of Democritus' thought we know from its presentation in the writings of Aristotle, who remains the most complete source of information regarding pre-Socratic Greek philosophy.

of these microscopic atoms moving within the void.

Thus we can see that over 2,400 years ago matter was proposed to be comprised of discrete particles that could be no further divided, and, because of this indivisibility, it was concluded that they must necessarily be internally homogeneous and atemporal. While there is much of Democritus' speculations that have failed to stand the test of time, his contention that the world is comprised of homogeneous elementary particles stands as one of the greatest scientific insights in human history. No other thought had ever been more ahead of its time.

As was the case in ancient Greece, ancient Indian philosophers also developed atomic theories of matter. Thinkers in the Buddhist school known as the Vaibhashika made similar insights to those of Democritus, namely that the world must be comprised of indivisible elementary particles. Just as in Greece, the theory of atomism was hotly contested in India. The Indian thinker Vasubandhu rejected the idea of objectively real indivisible atoms on the grounds that they could not account for the formation of objects experienced in the world. In the fourth century he produced a paradox to demonstrate this impossibility. The paradox can be described as follows.

Imagine a single atom alone in space. Then imagine six additional atoms, one directly above it, one directly below it, one on the left of it, one on the right of it, one in front, and one behind it. If it is true that atoms are homogeneous in their internal structure then we are forced to believe that, having no parts, they have no sides. For how could an indivisible homogeneous structure contain a top or a bottom, a right or a left? So in our example, the atom in the middle does not have a top that is facing the bottom of the atom directly above it. In other words, it is impossible to conceive of a relative position in space next to a homogeneous structure, as to face one side, or to interact with one side, must be the equivalent of interacting with all sides at once. Therefore the scenario of an atom surrounded on all sides by other atoms cannot even be thought of. It is as inconceivable as a circle that contains an angle or a square with five sides.

This seems like a devastating paradox, a proof that matter could not be comprised of indivisible homogeneous particles. However, we know that it is. But how can this be? How can our common sense notion of objective spatially extended physical reality be built from internally homogeneous elementary particles? The simple answer is that it cannot be. The paradox still holds true; you cannot have it both ways. However, instead of giving up on the idea of indivisible homogeneous elementary particles, as suggested by Vasubandhu, we instead need to give up on the notion of objective microphysical reality.

Idealism is the Consequence of Essesential Being

Whether considering the nature of elementary particles from an analytical or empirical perspective, homogeneity of internal content remains an inescapable feature. From an analytical perspective elementary particles are homogeneous by definition, for if they contained any differentiated internal structure then they would have parts, and then those parts should be considered elementary particles, not the whole that contains them. Empirically this conclusion of homogeneity is completely supported by the statistical accuracy of quantum mechanics[7], which works by forcing a limit to the subdivision of matter and energy.

Just as was the case with numbers, the direct result of elementary particles' homogeneity of internal content is their indistinguishability among others of the same type. A "down quark" is a "down quark". It is because they are each homogeneous in internal content that they lose the ability to be differentiated. There are zero differences between them. The fundamentality of this indistinguish-ability cannot be overstated, as the degree of ontological equivalence is far different from anything a person could experience in the macroscopic world. We need to be wary of analogies that obscure this fact. To illustrate, consider an unopened shipping case of a hundred sets of children's coloring crayons. In this case you know that there are exactly one hundred, never before used, red crayons. Are these red crayons distinguishable from each other? Practically, of course they are not, by just looking at them you could not tell them apart. However, if you increase the sophistication of your investigation you will find that these crayons are absolutely distinguishable. They may be identical to the untrained naked eye; however this is far from claiming that they are perfectly physically identical. There are of course many physical differences that would distinguish one red crayon from another. For example, every red crayon in the case, and likely every other red crayon in existence has a different total number of molecules in it.

---

[7] Quantum Mechanics refers to the mathematical processes that physicists use when dealing with elementary particles. I will forgo any further explanation at this point due to the fact that the next chapter will be entirely devoted to the topic.

Furthermore, the exact density of the molecules throughout the length of the body of each crayon are not, on the molecular level, absolutely uniform, neither are their chemical composition. The surfaces of each crayon are not as perfectly smooth as they look to the naked eye, but they are full of bumps and scratches too small to be seen, the exact placement of each is unique to the individual crayon. They are markers of its past.

Human minds have not evolved to think about quarks, electrons, or photons. They have evolved to think about macro physical objects like crayons, tree leaves, and bumble bees. This predisposes us to a cognitive bias. It makes it all too easy to jump to the conclusion that, although sometimes two things seem identical and indistinguishable from each other, in actuality they are not. Our default mode of reasoning, our cognitive bias, is to assume the distinguishability of all objects. However, unlike the crayons in our example, there simply is not a lower level where the differences between elementary particles of the same type will become apparent and distinguishability will be saved. We need to keep this fact in the fore front of our minds so that we can appreciate the strangeness of the great consequence that we now face. That is, beings that are internally homogeneous and indistinguishable from each other must also be atemporal as they cannot carry within themselves a history of their being, evidence of their existence over time. Unlike crayons, which based on the idiosyncrasies of their past, have specific bumps and scrapes on their surface, differences in their total mass and distribution of internal volume, elementary particles of the same type are perfectly identical in every conceivable way. Without an internal manifestation of their history they exist in their totality as

51

equivalent members of the same class (e.g., up quark, electron, etc.). There is no aspect of their existence that is beyond being a member of their class. Their being, like that of a number, is isomorphic to information regarding their class. They have no individual existence over time, and therefore, like a number, they should not be regarded as capable of independently persisting in time. They exist simply as information, nothing more.

To better summarize: the consequence of elementary particles' homogeneity is that they have no capacity for existing beyond their essence. Since the entirety of their existence is bound up in their essence, the potential for being over time, independent objective persistence, is precluded. This negative thesis is the first brick in the foundation of this idealism. In its simplest form it can be stated:

> Due to their internal homogeneity and indistinguishability, the elementary particles that comprise the matter and energy of the physical universe can have no independent objective persistence through time.

Much more needs to be added for certain, as a negative assertion does not equal a positive ontology. However, this negative assertion forms the foundation for all that will follow. In his doubt Descartes asserted that there are limitations to our certainty about our knowledge of the nature of objective physical reality. Going further, Berkley's Immaterialism asserts that there is no compelling evidence for the existence of an objective physical reality. These arguments were epistemologically based; they highlighted the limits of our ability to prove the existence and nature of physical reality. In contrast, the *essesential argument* presented here is an attempt to achieve an ontological foundation for idealism by providing the reason why the physical universe is not self-sustaining through time. That is: the physical universe is nothing but information, and information cannot objectively persist in time.

It may not be immediately obvious whether or not this last claim is true. You may be thinking why it should be impossible for information to objectively persist in time. In order to examine it more closely let us attempt to conceive of it as occurring in a possible world. Can we imagine a possible world in which there is no consciousness and in which there is no objectively persisting physical substance, a world in which there is only information? When I try to do this I am confronted with the simple fact that information without recourse to being recorded in a physical structure (e.g., pencil marks on paper, radio waves moving through the air) or registered in consciousness appears to be impossible. This is because without consciousness or the notion of objectively persisting physical objects there is nothing to constrain the hypothetical information to any degree of specificity. The information would immediately and spontaneously decohere; it would spread out and fill any and all possibilities. To illustrate, let us suppose that we were able to somehow put information into this possible world. Let us use the simple binary string 0010. Without recourse to consciousness or physical objects there is nothing to stop that 0010 from becoming 0011 or perhaps 0000, or 1111. Information isolated from other being loses is specificity. Indeed there is nothing to stop it from existing as 00000111010101110101, or 101^{839}, or the binary code to Michael Jackson's *Thriller*. Information simply cannot be thought to exist without recourse to some external structure (objectively persisting physical objects or consciousness). Yes, technically I can conceive of a possible world without consciousness or objectively existing physical things. And yes, I could imagine that there is information in that world. However, as was just mentioned any information in that world would spread itself out to the edge of possibility, simultaneously exhibiting mutually exclusive manifestations of itself. It would cease to be information as we define and understand it. Therefore such a world cannot be our current world.

When physicists talk about the possibility that physical reality may be at its core information based (e.g., Tegmark, 2014; Wheeler, 1990) they invariably skip over this problem. They appear to not see it as a problem. Maybe this is due to an overtly mathematical orientation or an allegiance to a type of platonic mathematical realism. I can't be sure. Regardless of the reason, it is surely an error to do so. The problem must be acknowledged. Whether one calls it, *it from bit*, *the mathematical universe hypothesis*, or if they choose to characterize it as I do with the term *essesential being*, the fact remains that if physical reality is not comprised of inert substance but of information, then we are left with the simple fact that this information cannot exist as it does without the presence of something else. Without recourse to objectively existing physical things there is only one option remaining: consciousness.

4

Idealism Explains Quantum Mechanics

But enough of this philosophizing and logical trickery you may say. The arguments presented in the last chapter are not going to make me change my beliefs about the nature of reality. Even while conceding that the essesential nature of elementary particles appears to leave them without the capability to persist independently in time, you may also be thinking that there has to be another way out. There must still be an objective micro physical reality. The alternative is simply too strange an idea to seriously entertain. Certainly modern empirical physics would disagree with the preceding nonsense, right? It may surprise you to find out that there is not a simple answer to this question. Opinions vary, and it would be disingenuous to pretend otherwise. This chapter will be devoted to trying to explain exactly what physics has to say on the matter, what has actually been discovered along with how physicists have been struggling to interpret the meaning of these empirical facts.

In physics, the mathematical procedures known as quantum mechanics, which have perfectly described the results of every experiment regarding elementary particles ever done, work in a way that does not allow for elementary particles to have objective being over time. This is the only way the math works. By using the term quantum mechanics physicists are distinguishing it from the old classical mechanics, the mathematical machinery of Isaac Newton and James Clark Maxwell. The difference is that in classical mechanics matter and energy are treated as if they were continuous, without end to their divisibility. In contrast, in quantum mechanics matter and energy's divisibility is limited; there is a smallest part to each that cannot be further divided. This new mathematical machinery was forced upon physicists in the early 20th century who needed it to deal with the discrete nature of elementary particles. Quantum mechanics has turned out to be astoundingly accurate. It has therefore replaced classical mechanics as the foundational mechanics in physics. Today it stands as the bedrock of physical science and the foundation of our modern technology.

To be clear, there is no practical or technological problem with quantum mechanics. In this regard things have been working perfectly for decades. There is, however, a conceptual problem. The problem is that quantum mechanics works in a way that is counter to our everyday understanding. It requires us to let go of the rules that we assume nature has to play by, rules such as the idea that an object cannot be in two places at once, or that there can be no element of randomness in the outcome of basic physical interactions. Such incongruence with these seemingly unassailable truths of physical logic makes quantum mechanics difficult to accept. To help his students get over this dissonance, Richard Feynman, one of the most prominent physicists of the twentieth century, famously gave the following advice:

> "I am going to tell you what nature behaves like. If you will simply admit that maybe she does behave like this, you will find her a delightful, entrancing thing. Do not keep saying to yourself, if

you can possibly avoid it, "But how can it be like
that?" because you will get 'down the drain', into a
blind alley from which nobody has escaped. Nobody knows how it can be like that."

Feynman was referring to what is known as the "measurement problem", the central conceptual puzzle in quantum mechanics. In the old classical view every particle was
thought to have, at every moment, an exact position and
an exact momentum. These values were thought to change
deterministically over time according to Newton's laws.
However, in quantum mechanics particles do not have exactly determined properties, and when they are measured,
the result appears to be randomly drawn from a probability
distribution. In 1926 the physicist Erwin Schrödinger published an equation that shows how these probability distri-
butions are determined but cannot predict the exact result
of any one measurement. This equation ranks as one of
physic's greatest achievements, as it seems to represent the
workings of physical reality at its most basic level.

Initially Schrödinger's interpretation of his seminal
equation was that it described the waves that comprised
matter. However, wave mechanics of this kind did not ultimately fit the data. It was the physicist Max Born who
quickly realized that what Schrödinger's equation actually
does is provide the probabilities of finding a particular
measurement outcome. This insight, along with the theoretical work of Niels Bohr and Werner Heisenberg, became
known as the Copenhagen Interpretation of quantum mechanics. This interpretation holds that before measurement particles exist as a collection of all their possible

states, known as the superposition. It is the act of measurement itself that "collapses" the wave function into only one of these possible states. So when a measurement is taken we get an answer regarding a particle's state, the state that the experiment was designed to measure (e.g., spin, position, momentum, etc.). However, the Copenhagen Interpretation would have us believe that Schrödinger's wave function actually describes the extent of what can be known in between measurements. Taken seriously, this means believing in the reality of the superposition, particles existing in multiple places with multiple mutually exclusive properties at the same time. It also requires believing that at the very moment when a scientist decides to take a measurement that he forces nature to choose, at random, only one of the possibilities to manifest itself. If what you have just read seems impossible, a violation of basic physical logic, then you are in good company. Bohr himself acknowledged, "For those who are not shocked when they first come across quantum theory cannot possibly have understood it."

Despite his great contribution, Erwin Schrödinger refused to accept the Copenhagen Interpretation of quantum mechanics. He is famously quoted as lamenting, "I don't like it, and I'm sorry I ever had anything to do with it." In 1935 he devised a clever thought experiment to demonstrate just how absurd the notion of superposition was. This has since become known as Schrödinger's cat. Imagine a cat that is sealed in a soundproof box. In the box with the cat is a vile of poison strong enough to kill the cat if it were to be broken. Also inside this hideous box is an experimental apparatus that will detect some random quantum event, such as whether or not a radioactive atom has decayed. Lastly, let us suppose that a mechanical device is attached the experimental apparatus so that if the atom were to emit radiation a tiny spring loaded hammer would be released breaking the vile of poison and killing the cat. Conversely, if the atom had yet to emit any radiation then nothing would happen and the cat would survive. According to the Copenhagen Interpretation the atom's decay is a probabilistic event that will, after a certain amount of time, be just as likely to have occurred as to not. At this point before measurement the Copenhagen Interpretation would have us believe that the cat would be in a superposition between both a dead and an alive state; it would be both alive and dead at the same time. Only when the experimenter opens up the box and looks inside will the superposition finally collapse and the cat will be forced into either a dead or an alive state. Even stranger still, consider that once the measurement took place the cat would have been dead completely or alive completely during the interim of time before the experimenter looked into the box. So looking back at it in time the period of superposition would have disappeared. What this demonstrates is that taking the Copenhagen Interpretation at face value means the act of measurement (observation) by the experimenter actually changes the past.

Examining the situation more closely you may ask the question what is measurement? Is it merely the particles' interaction with the physical measurement devise? But, is not the measurement devise itself comprised of particles that are also subject to the Schrödinger equation? Therefore, should we not consider the measurement devise itself, like Schrödinger's cat, to also be in a state of superposition? Now take it one more step further and consider what would happen if the physicist who was conducting an experiment had their friend, who does not have a PhD in physics, look at the instrument display first. Can we then consider the particle about to be measured, the physical measurement devise, and the mind and body of this friend all in a state of superposition until the physicist asks him what he saw on the instrument display? This seems insane. Shouldn't common sense dictate that consciousness cannot be in a state of superposition? And why should a PhD in physics have anything to do with it? These questions were posed by the physicist Eugene Wigner and have come to be known as Wigner's friend paradox. Wigner, building off of the insights of the great mathematician John von Neumann (1932) suggested a simple but profound augmentation to the Copenhagen Interpretation (Wigner, 1961). This has since become known as the Consciousness Causes Collapse Interpretation of quantum mechanics.

This Consciousness Causes Collapse interpretation contends that there is no logical or empirical way in which to differentiate between the particles being measured and the measurement devise. Being physical, they are all subject to exist in superposition. Instead it is the wave function's interaction with consciousness itself that causes its collapse. This is because consciousness, being nonphysical, is not governed by the Schrödinger equation. It cannot be in a state of superposition. It is outside of the dynamics. The arrival of the Consciousness Causes Collapse Interpretation of quantum mechanics constitutes a watershed moment for idealism. For the first time in history, from a wholly scientific perspective, consciousness was postulated to hold a foundational place in the nature of reality. Unfortunately, this profound conjecture has been almost completely ignored by contemporary physicists. The implications for them, I believe, are simply unacceptable.

We have just traveled a great distance in a short time. So that we do not get too far ahead of ourselves, allow me to clarify what is fact from what is interpretation. There is no disagreement in physics as to whether or not the Schrödinger equation describes and predicts experimental results with 100 percent accuracy. This is an empirical fact of science. The mathematics works perfectly; it has never been wrong. In fact, as mentioned earlier, it working the way that it does underpins our modern world, everything from MRI machines to superconductors to smart phones. The big question, where there is ample disagreement among physicists, is why and how could it possibly work? At a conceptual level, what must reality be like for it to work? How could any degree of indeterminacy exist at the fundamental level of the physical universe? How could particles be in two places at once, or simultaneously manifest mutually exclusive properties? Why should measurement be so important? It is clear that the Copenhagen Interpretation of quantum mechanics forbids the notion of independently persisting elementary particles. But is this interpretation of the mathematical machinery correct? Is something being missed? Can the old conceptualization of a deterministic universe where particles do not exist as potentialities in multiple places at once be saved?

Einstein's Objection: The EPR Paradox

Albert Einstein hated the conclusions that quantum mechanics seemed to be forcing on the physicists of his day. Instead he preferred a wholly objective and deterministic universe. In response to the inherent randomness at the heart of quantum theory he famously exclaimed that "God does not play dice". Einstein was convinced that there were "hidden variables", variables that physicists had not yet discovered that were objectively determining the results of each quantum measurement. He thought that the eventual discovery of these hidden variables by future physicists would explain why the measurement outcomes appeared to have a degree of randomness to them even though they were completely determined by their previous state. Einstein never produced an account of what these variables could be or how they might one day be measured. His belief in them appeared to have been constructed from the distaste he had for the alternative. The quantum mechanical picture of reality had to be wrong, or at least incomplete, because it ran counter to his assumptions on what reality must be.

In 1935 Albert Einstein, along with Boris Podolsky and Nathan Rosen, published a paper entitled, "Can the Quantum-Mechanical Description of Physical Reality be Considered Complete?". Based on the names of its three authors the content of this famous paper has since become known as the EPR paradox. The paper presented an ingenious thought experiment that was aimed at convincing the physics community that the Schrödinger equation could not possibly describe physical reality. Their argument can be summarized as follows. Suppose a pair of complimentary photons were created in a lab so that one of the photons must have an "up" spin and the other a "down" spin. These twin photons would be considered to be *entangled* with one another; their shared past would require them to manifest complimentary characteristics when measured (e.g., they cannot both have up spins).

Einstein questioned what would happen if one of the photons stayed in the lab awaiting measurement while the other photon left the building and traveled to the other end of the galaxy. According to the standard interpretation of quantum mechanics, he contends, we are asked to believe that both photons are in a state of superposition (i.e., simultaneously manifesting both an up and a down spin) until the act of measurement forces them to take on either one or the other characteristic. Now let us suppose that one particular day at an arbitrary time one of the laboratory technicians decides on a whim to measure the photon in the lab, finding that it has an up spin. Then Einstein asks are we supposed to believe that at the exact moment this measurement is taken billions of miles away there is an instantaneous change in the state of the second photon so that it is now compelled to manifest a down spin. Being billions of miles away how does the photon even know that the measurement has occurred in the lab, let alone what state it must collapse into so that it can be congruent with its twin? How can a photon know anything?

Einstein famously referred to this type of nonlocal influence as "spooky action at a distance". He made this characterization because such non-locality is at odds with the very idea of spatially extended physical reality. In his mind it would be almost unnatural, hence "spooky". What Einstein clearly understood was that the Schrödinger equation prohibited nothing less than localized physical reality itself, which is why he did not believe it to be a complete picture of the dynamics. The aim of his paper was to convince others that the implications of quantum mechanics were so absurd that they could not possibly be correct. At

63

the time it was written, however, it was just a thought experiment; time had to pass before physicists were able to get a handle on how to explore this paradox experimentally. Einstein would not live to see the outcome. He died in 1955.

In 1964, nearly thirty years after the publication of the EPR paradox, the Irish theoretical physicist John Bell developed a method to actually test it. He presented an inequality that could be used to differentiate whether the results of a series of quantum measurements had the element of actual chance as would be predicted by quantum mechanics, or if hidden variables could be producing results that merely seemed probabilistic. This inequality provided physicists with the needed mathematical apparatus to test whether Einstein was right about there being an objective reality that underpinned the apparent randomness and non locality. Bell, however, would have to wait until the 1980's before technological advances made it possible for his theorem to be used in an actual experiment.

In 1981, a team lead by the French physicist Allan Aspect published the first empirical tests of the EPR paradox (Aspect, Grangier, & Roger, 1981; Aspect, Dalibard, & Roger, 1982). To the surprise of many, clear violations of Bell's inequalities were found, thus effectively ruling out the class of local hidden variable theories. Using pairs of entangled photons it was found that the act of measuring one of the pair limits the possibilities of the state of the other photon to a state that would show consistency with the first measurement. Furthermore, it did not matter that in this experiment the settings on the measurement devise were changed after the photons were separated. Somehow the photons still "knew" what state they had to manifest in order to show consistency with their twin. In the decades since, these results have been replicated many times and over increasingly farther distances. In 1998, pairs of entangled photons demonstrated consistency with their twin despite being separated between two Swiss villages nearly 11 kilometers apart (Tittel et al, 1998). To achieve this, any type of "spooky action at a distance" would have to have been propagated at more than 20,000 times the speed of light. Going even further, researchers measured pairs of entangled photons that had been bounced off of a satellite at a distance of nearly 144 kilometers (Ursin et al, 2007). As was the case with all the previous experiments, Bells inequalities were violated. Further upping the stakes, Gröblacher (et al, 2007) and his team changed certain features of the methodology that allowed them to conduct experiments on sets of entangled photons that excluded a large class of even non local hidden variables. Unlike earlier experiments, by starting to exclude the influence of non local hidden variables, realism itself is set on shaky ground. There appears to be no other way to interpret the findings. They write:

> "Most working scientists hold fast to the concept of 'realism' - a viewpoint according to which an external reality exists independent of observation. But quantum physics has shattered some of our cornerstone beliefs…...Our result suggests that giving up the concept of locality is not sufficient to be consistent with quantum experiments, unless certain intuitive features of realism are abandoned"

Tests of the EPR paradox have left us in a world where the Copenhagen concepts of superposition and indeterminacy, along with their most counterintuitive consequence, non-locality, have been empirically validated. Therefore, if Einstein was correct that was the final nail in the coffin for physical realism. Objective microphysical reality does not exist. What Einstein believed to be an obvious impossibility is now an empirical fact of science. Although for an idealist these results are not at all troubling. They are only a conundrum for those who hold an a priori commitment to materialism and objective realism. These are the ones that are asking, "But how can it be like that?" However, if one views elementary particles as holding on to no being outside of their essence, then there is no problem. Particles are information and information can easily change to demonstrate consistency in entanglement. It is just information; it exists for consciousness. Of course, by starting with different assumptions, physicists can still derive theoretical frameworks that seem to preserve realism to varying degrees. We shall see this in the next section where the Many Worlds Interpretation of quantum mechanics is discussed. However, to accomplish this requires a lot of wrangling and is fraught with extra, immeasurable, elements that need to be added into reality to make it work. The fact remains, taken at face value, the tests of the EPR paradox have consistently provided evidence congruent with idealism and in contrast to the notion of an objective spatially extended physical reality.

The Interpretations of Quantum Mechanics

There are several general classes of what are called interpretations of quantum mechanics. These interpretations can be thought of as attempts to answer the question, "But how can it be like that?". None of these interpretations can restore the classical picture of objective physical reality, and none of them appear to enjoy a clear majority of support within the physics community (Schlosshauer, et al, 2013). While it would be wrong to say that determining which interpretation is correct is something that is outside the realm of scientific investigation, it is certainly accurate to say that the question has a very large philosophical component to it. Which interpretation one prefers is heavily dependent on their assumptions of what reality must be like. Suffice it to say, that is why there is such differing opinion.

In what follows I will touch on the two leading mainstream interpretations[8] as they are generally understood (The Copenhagen Interpretation and Everett's Many Worlds Hypothesis) and compare them to the von Neumann/Wigner augmentation to the Copenhagen Interpretation, the Consciousness Causes Collapse Interpretation. I will not pretend that this is an unbiased review. I will admit at the onset that I think that the Consciousness Causes Collapse Interpretation is the correct viewpoint. It

---

[8] There are many alternative interpretations of Quantum Mechanics outside of the Copenhagen Interpretation and the Many Worlds Interpretation. A short list of them may include The Consistent Histories Interpretation (Griffiths, 1984), the de Broglie–Bohm Pilot Wave Theory (Bohm, 1952), the Ensemble Interpretation (Ballentine, 1970), Relational Quantum Mechanics (Rovelli, 1996), and the objective collapse interpretation (Penrose, 1989). Since this is a book about idealism and not quantum mechanics it would have been too distracting to describe these in the text.

is the only interpretation that is consistent with idealism, and in my view, nearly mandates it. It is not too great a stretch to conjecture that this fact is what makes such a simple and obvious solution so unpalatable to physicists, whom I presume, unlike myself, would want nothing at all to do with idealism.

The Copenhagen Interpretation

The Copenhagen Interpretation was the first attempt to translate the mathematical structure of quantum mechanics into everyday language. Since the 1920's when it was fiercely championed by Werner Heisenberg and Niels Bohr it has become the orthodox interpretation of quantum mechanics. Although there is not a singular document that lays out explicitly what the Copenhagen Interpretation is, its central tenant is that the superposition is an accurate representation of all that can be known of the physical reality in between measurements. The consequences of this, the loss of local realism and complete physical determinism are acknowledged. The Copenhagen Interpretation is minimalist in nature. It just takes the apparent empirical facts of what is observed (the loss of local realism and the loss of physical determinism) at face value. It does not try to explain the reality behind the scenes. In the Copenhagen Interpretation there is no hidden reality. It contends that the wave function collapses to a single state upon measurement but is silent on how or why this should occur. The paradoxes that arise from this such as the EPR paradox, Schrödinger's Cat, or Wigner's Friend are simply accepted. One could even say that Copenhagen is in a sense a lack of an interpretation as it seems to provide no deeper answers as to the meaning of quantum theory. None of the *why* questions are answered. Despite this, or perhaps because of it, the Copenhagen Interpretation remains the standard interpretation of quantum mechanics.

The Many Worlds Interpretation

In 1957 Hugh Everett published a paper that originated from his doctoral dissertation entitled "Relative State Formulation of Quantum Mechanics'. In this seminal paper he argues that the Schrödinger equation should not be seen has containing a probability wave that collapses upon measurement. He thought this to be the wrong description of physical reality. Instead of just one actual occurrence probabilistically arising from many potentialities, he contended that every one of those potentialities actually occurs. In other words, the wave function never collapses. Whenever two particles interact every possible state that might occur actually does occur. He hypothesized that instead of reality consisting of only one universe, that there exists a nearly infinite number of parallel universes. Every particle interaction simply causes them to diverge from a shared pre-measurement state so that each possible outcome is manifested in a separate universe. In the Schrödinger's cat paradigm the cat survives in one universe only to die in another. From the perspective of any one of these universes the results of a quantum measurement would seem random, as we find ourselves in just one of the universes. This is how the Many Worlds Interpretation gets around the randomness problem, and answers Einstein's objection that God does not play dice. This is the primary strength of this interpretation; it appears to keep physics fully deterministic. Everett's ideas were later championed by Dewitt (1970) who coined the term the Many Worlds Interpretation. This view is currently espoused by a growing number of contemporary physicists (e.g., Deutsch, 1999; Tegmark, 2014) who see it as a workable alternative to the Copenhagen Interpretation.

However, while Everett's God does not play dice, he never makes a decision either. In the Many Worlds Interpretation literally everything happens; there is nothing that does not happen. When particles interact every possibility is manifested. In a sense it is not really determinism at all. Nothing is determined one way or another because nature never makes a decision. This seems like a cop out, a clever trick of reasoning in that it sneaks out of answering any "why" questions by asserting that everything relies on anthropomorphic chance. Everett and subsequent Many Worlds enthusiast are also silent on the mechanism that gives birth to the relentless divergence of reality? This is a big issue, maybe even a fatal flaw. What is the point of trading in one mystery for another, especially one with an ontological premise far more bizarre than the problem that it was designed to remedy.

Although I disagree with it, I find Everett's hypothesis to be a work of profound creativity and genius. He found a way to save the physical world for physics. No collapse means no Wigner's Friend paradox; all notions of observation or consciousness are removed from the picture. However, the fact that any physicist believes in such a speculation is telling of the lengths that a discipline will go through to retain control of their subject matter (i.e., to keep consciousness out). When pressed, a physicist, if he or she chooses to answer, has a limited number of options to interpret the Schrödinger equation. To accept the original

Copenhagen Interpretation is a half measure, a cop out, because it provides no interpretive foundation for the theory. It provides only paradoxes without answering fundamental questions (i.e., what is measurement and why should it collapse the wave function, how is the measurement devise different from the quantum phenomena under study, how could there be any randomness in fundamental physical theory, and how is non locality even conceivable within a spatially extended physical reality). This leaves Everett's hypothesis as the leading other means to keep physics as the foundation of all knowledge and existence. I suspect that this is the only reason it receives any support at all. However, I speculate that a third wishful thinking option remains that allows the conscience of the discipline to remain in acceptance of the Copenhagen Interpretation's unfulfilling void of explanation, that is the idea that a new solution will one day become available that will explain why the Schrödinger equation works without resulting to a belief in an infinite number of divergent universes. This implicit belief keeps the conceptual dissonance at bay and allows physics to ignore the simplest and most parsimonious answer, the answer suggested long ago by von Neumann and Wigner, which is that the particle's interaction with consciousness is the mechanism that collapses the wave function.

The Consciousness Causes Collapse Interpretation

The consciousness causes collapse interpretation is the natural completion of the Copenhagen Interpretation. It simply accepts the Schrödinger equation to be a complete description of physical reality and then contends that collapse occurs at the point of interaction with a conscious observer. In the decades since its inception scientists from a variety of disciplines have argued for the validity of this interpretation and have attempted to develop it and apply it further (Beck & Eccles, 1998; d'Espagnat, 1979; Goswami, 1993/2008; Lanza & Berman, 2009; Schwartz & Begley, 2002; Stapp, 2005; Walker, 1998). As mentioned earlier, in this interpretation it is not the measurement devise but the interaction of consciousness itself with the physical system that results in the collapse of the wave function. This resolves the Wigner's friend paradox (the first person who sees the result causes collapse) it also resolves the Schrödinger's cat paradox (the cat's experience or non-experience of the poison causes collapse). It does all of this without the need for an incalculable number of divergent universes, which makes it far more parsimonious than Everett's hypothesis. However, in order to entertain this interpretation you have to let consciousness into physics. I cannot imagine how distasteful that must be for physicists, considering that most psychologists barely want to include it into scientific psychology. The pressure to dismiss it out of hand as obviously false must be enormous.

This Consciousness Causes Collapse Interpretation is hated by the majority of physicist who write about it and it has been lampooned with impassioned distain. Its rate of adherence in a recent survey of physicists, philosophers, and mathematicians was found to be at only six percent of respondents, far below Copenhagen's 42 percent or the Many World's 18 percent (Schlosshauer et al, 2013).

Objections to this view can be reduced to two central points of contention. These arguments can be characterized as the *parsimony argument* and the *how argument*. The parsimony argument against the Consciousness Causes Collapse Interpretation is predicated on the assumption that consciousness should not have anything to do with the workings of physical reality. In other words by bringing consciousness into physics things are complicated unnecessarily. I do not think this argument has merit. If one assumes that science would have to someday and somehow account for consciousness and include it in to a complete description of the natural world then the parsimony argument disappears. The parsimony argument only exists if one has an *a priori* commitment to materialism. Therefore it is not a sufficient reason to reject the hypothesis, especially considering that there are good independent reasons to doubt that materialism is the correct metaphysical position.

In contrast to the parsimony argument, the second common objection; the question of *how* could this be the case is legitimate and needs explaining. In other words, *how* can the basic mechanism of physical reality work in a way that would depend on consciousness, something that we have no evidence of existing at the onset of the universe, something that requires billions of years of star and planet formation along will hundreds of millions of years of biological evolution to exist? If physical reality requires consciousness then how could it have existed for billions of years without it? Furthermore, it should be acknowledged that from the perspective of materialism the Consciousness Causes Collapse Interpretation does not make any sense. It only works if one agrees that consciousness is something nonphysical so that it exists outside of the Schrödinger equation. This brings us to the next *how* question. How could something nonphysical effect something physical? How could consciousness cause the wave function to collapse? There appears to be no imaginable way for this to occur, at least no way that is currently understood in the sciences. So therefore what reason is there to even consider the Consciousness Causes Collapse Interpretation in the face of such road blocks? These *how* questions are difficult, and, despite their great insights, von Neumann and Wigner did not provide us with any satisfactory answers. However, I think that a serious consideration of an idealist, rather than a dualist, metaphysics can provide satisfactory answers to these *how* questions regarding this interpretation, as well as address the broader question of why superpositions should exist in the first place. An attempt at answering these questions will be the focus of the following two chapters. However, the path that this proposed solution will take can be briefly outlined here.

At the end of the last chapter it was argued that the physical universe is nothing but information, and information cannot objectively persist in time without something else supporting its being. The problem identified with information existing independently would be that there would be nothing to constrain the hypothetical information to any degree of specificity. The information would immediately and spontaneously decohere. It would spread out and fill any and all possibilities, simultaneously exhibiting mutually exclusive manifestations of itself. It will be argued that this information in isolation is quantum superposition. This superposition exists until something external to it forces it to a degree of specificity so that it can be consistent with the larger entanglements. That external "something" is consciousness. In the next chapter it will be argued that consciousness is not doomed to exist as information the way that the components of the physical universe are. I hope to demonstrate that consciousness, unlike the elementary particles that comprise the physical universe, can hold on to existence beyond its essence; it can escape its essence and persist in time. It therefore becomes the being by which persistence over time enters reality. This persistence over time is what allows it to form entanglements with the essesential being of which the physical universe is comprised.

5
Consciousness is Existential Being

"Existence is precisely the opposite of finality."

- Soren Kierkegaard, *Concluding Unscientific Postscript*, 1846

In the preceding chapters we seemed to have stripped reality of its being, of its manifest presence. To reiterate, it was argued that if we were to consider that physical reality is all that there is, while simultaneously contending that this physical reality exists only as a pattern of information, a mathematical object, then we are left to conclude that what we call reality is nothing more than an abstraction that cannot exist on its own. Since this cannot be the case, and we cannot get this from information alone, we are left to ask how does reality obtain its raw presence, its manifestation, its being? How does it get its existence?

But let us first step back and consider the most basic question. What is *existence* itself, what is *being*? Unfortunately this question is out of the realm of science and has been deemed unimportant by contemporary analytical philosophy. Throughout its history, science's quest for knowledge has been focused on the extrinsic facts of observation, properties of things and how they related to other properties (i.e., the essence of things). It has all been quite rational, and even, such as in the case of quantum mechanics and theoretical physics in general, quite mathematical. For more than 2000 years the emphasis in western thought has been placed primarily on essence, and it was assumed that once mastery was obtained over the essence of things that "being" would present itself on the cheap, or worse yet, that once you understand the essence of a thing then its being becomes an unnecessary appendage, a meaningless predicate. This hyper focus on understanding essence blinds us from appreciating the phenomenology of existence itself. This "existence" is what holds the extrinsic facts of observation together. Without existence there can be no extrinsic properties and relations for science to explore, without existence there is no essence, no information. Simply phrased, existence must be understood as separate from essence, as prior to essence. The great existentialist philosophers[9] of the 19th and 20th century: Soren Kierkegaard (1813-1855), Martin Heidegger (1889-1976), and Jean Paul Sartre (1905-1980), warn us of neglecting this simple fact. However, their warnings have fallen on death ears. The pillars of contemporary ontological theorizing (e.g., string theory, eliminative materialism, multiple universes) fail to acknowledge what ought to be their starting point, the phenomena of existence itself.

To help clarify the distinction between existence and essence I will rely on an analogy already given by Sartre. Consider a paper cutter. The essence of a paper cutter is its functionality as a simple machine that cuts paper. It may also be of a particular design, size, brand name, color etc. These properties are all constituents of the essence of the

---

[9] The philosophy of existentialism, like any other school or movement, contains divergent thought among its adherents. To be sure there are parts of Sartre's philosophy that would mortify Kierkegaard and likely vice versa. What I want to talk about is not the particularity of any one existentialist thinker, but the thread that holds them together, the core principle that existence precedes essence, that it is ontologically separate from essence. To recognize this, and to bring it to the forefront of one's thinking, is to be an existentialist, a philosopher of existence.

paper cutter. In manufacturing, essence precedes existence. There first exists an idea of the paper cutter, a formal design plan, blueprints that then become manufactured into individual paper cutters. The essence of a thing, its properties, come before its existence. Ever since Plato's theory of the "forms" 2,400 years ago this has been the underlying current of western philosophy. The emphasis has been on understanding the essence, the abstraction, of things rather than focusing on their existence, that which is beyond their essence. To understand circular objects you need to know $C=\pi(d)$, to understand the power of a thrown rock you need to know $v=dr/dt$, and to understand the equivalence of matter and energy you need to know $E=mc^2$. However, we readily overlook how any of this could manifest itself in being, how its existence could actually occur. By staring so intently at the abstraction of a thing we look right past its existence, as a consequence "being" itself becomes lost.

Existentialism views things from the opposite perspective. *Being* is put first. The focus is placed on the subjective phenomenology of the existing now. At its heart, existentialism recognizes the impossibility of fully capturing "being" in any type of systematic thought, of ever reducing an existing phenomenon entirely to its essence. In other words, it is an error to think that you can make an ontological flow chart, a schematic of being. Existence cannot be abstracted in such a way. It is indeed the opposite of abstraction because existence itself has no essence. The reason for this is that being, the existing now, is perpetually incomplete, which consequently makes it irreducible to information, to its essence. It is only once being has ended, once it has passed and is no longer incomplete, does it become reducible to its essence. Heidegger reminds us that this way of thinking was present in Heraclitus' ancient dictum that to be is to be in a constant state of becoming. Sartre characterizes it by stating that being lacks an equivalency with itself. It is this ceaseless state of becoming, this perpetual incompleteness, this lack of self equivalence at the heart of being that precludes the possibility of it ever achieving a full equivalency with information.

In the philosophy of Kierkegaard the being that preceded essence was the individual human, for Sartre the view was at times expanded to include humanity as a whole. Their focus, while at times ontological, remained centered on what this means for a person trying to live their life. In contrast to these philosophies, I will advocate for a much narrower focus. While I think that the overall concept of existence preceding essence is of paramount importance, I want to apply it differently. I disagree that the analysis should be at the level of humanity as a whole, or even the individual human life or human ego. Instead the focus needs to be on each individual moment of consciousness, as it is in these moments that we will find the ontological machinery necessary for consciousness to escape its essence and hold on to, ever briefly, being over time. What I wish to demonstrate in this chapter is that, unlike elementary particles whose existence is completely contained within their essence, each individual moment of consciousness is an example of existential being, a being that escapes its own essence, a being that exists beyond it. This is what separates consciousness ontologically from matter. Physical things exist only as essence (their defining information), while consciousness always exists beyond its essence through its irreducibility and being over time.

How to Exist Beyond Essence

Consciousness' escape from essence is a result of two structures of its being, its temporality and its irreducible experiential quality, the second being a direct consequence of the first. Let us first consider the temporality of consciousness, as in this structure we find the means towards its irreducibility. In doing so we are immediately confronted with a temporal discrepancy between the being of consciousness and the essesential brain processes with which it is correlated. Consciousness cannot be subdivided in time the way that physical processes can be. For example, there are physical processes that can occur in far less than a trillionth of a second. The smallest unit of physical time measured to date was 12 attoseconds (an attosecond is to a second what a second is to about 31 billion years). The physical processes in your brain are occurring in just as finely sliced infinitesimal spaces of time. The human brain is comprised of about 100 billion individual nerve cells called neurons. These neurons are thought to process information by communicating with other neurons through a process called synaptic transmission. In this process electrical signals traveling along each neuron are converted to chemical signals that jump to receiving neurons, which then initiate their own electrical signal. There are different types of neurons, and consequently different firing rates. Some fire upwards of 50 times a second. In each and every one of these firings there is an electrical signal that travels from one end of the neuron to the other. Keep in mind that there is nothing magical about this electrical signal. It is simply the movement of charged particles along the length of nerve cells. It is matter in motion, and as such, its path can be subdivided into unimaginably small units of time (i.e., trillionths of a second).

In contrast, consciousness cannot be so finely subdivided in time. There is a temporal limit to human awareness. In other words, consciousness requires a minimum amount of time to exist; it cannot exist in infinitesimally small frames. For example, two sequential flashes of light appear to consciousness as occurring simultaneously if the time lapse between them is small enough (Allport, 1968; Stroud, 1955). Such findings have lead some researchers to conclude that perception (consciousness) is best conceived of as being discrete rather than continuous, with an estimated duration of about one tenth of a second or more (Herzog, Kammer, & Scharnowski, 2016; VanRullen & Koch, 2003). Although neuroscience is still working out the details regarding discrete vs. continuous perception (Fingelkurts & Fingelkurts, 2006), it still remains an empirical fact of science, that humans cannot discriminate infinitesimal moments of time. There is no "red experience" or "cold experience" or "c sharp minor experience" that can exist in a billionth of a second, a millionth of a second, or even a thousandth of a second. There is a minimum duration of conscious experience that cannot be further subdivided. Therefore we are forced to conceptualize this chunk of time, this temporal extension of consciousness, as being internally homogenous. This puts consciousness in stark contrast to essesential being. Matter and energy are infinitesimal, having no existence over time, while temporal extensions of consciousness hold on to their unique and distinguishable existence over a definite span of time. Consciousness has duration. This being over time is the first step in consciousness' escape from its essence.

The irreducibility of the experiential content of consciousness, which finally allows it to escape its essence, is a necessary consequence of its temporally extended nature. Consider that at any one point within a temporal extension of consciousness, its experiential content must necessarily exist as an indivisible unity of being; the infinite totality of the physical points of time must exist as experientially co-occurring equals. Any attempt to completely correlate the experiential content with its essesential information would necessitate a correlation of nothing less than the totality of the frames existing during the entire temporal extension. However, such a complete equivalence could only be possible once the temporal extension has past. This means that the existence over time of the experiential content literally precedes the completion of its correlate essence, thus demonstrating the existentialist dictum that existence precedes essence.

To further illustrate, consider the conscious experience of seeing a red apple flashed on a computer screen. Past research informs us that the experience of seeing such an object is an event that at minimum requires about 50 milliseconds (a twentieth of a second) to occur. Your conscious perception of that red object is an all or nothing event, either you see it or you don't. The seeing it is supported by neurobiological activity (i.e., electrical signals traveling down the length of neurons and chemical signals activating electrical signals in subsequent neurons). Since physical time is greatly more divisible than consciousness, there would exist an innumerable amount of neurobiological snap shots in time for each indivisible chunk of red consciousness. In other words, this all or nothing conscious experience of red is an internally homogeneous and indivisible event that is supported in its being by an incalculable number of neurobiological snap shots. One may ask which slice of physical time underwrites the experience of red. What neurobiological moment "is" red? Is it the frame of time *"x"*, or is it a ten thousandth of a second later during frame *"y"*, or maybe the next snap shot over in frame *"z"*? The answer is that it is all of them. Each indivisible moment of consciousness, or temporal extension of consciousness, requires the entire relevant sequence of neurobiological events occurring within the duration of the interval. Since this will not happened until the end of the temporal extension, we can assert that throughout the duration of a moment of consciousness, the creation of a complete neurobiological equivalence is impossible. It can therefore be concluded that during the length of a temporal extension of consciousness, while it has live existence, it is in principle irreducible to its neurobiological underpinnings, to its essence.

This is why the quality of experience is so hard to pin down. It simply cannot be reduced to information. The hard problem of consciousness that David Chalmers alludes to will never be solved. The explanatory gap is an inescapable consequence of the fact that consciousness is compelled to exist beyond its own essence (the neuro-activity that supports it). Its nature is to exist in a constant state of becoming. What the great existentialist thinkers attributed to reality as a whole originates from the irreducibility of consciousness itself.

To summarize, we can say that consciousness that is currently existing is always in a mode of irreducibility to its essence. It becomes its essence only once it has past, but while it is existing, it is always beyond its essence, because no complete correlation is possible until the completion of the temporal extension. Thus we can think of consciousness as being relentlessly projected into the immediate future, constantly leaving its essence, the neural activity that supports it, behind.

Since, during its life span, each temporal extension of consciousness exists beyond its essence, it can be considered an example of *existential being,* a being that has existence over time. Existential being appears to be a necessary constituent of reality, as without it we are only left with essesential being (i.e., information), which cannot exist on its own. However, existential being also seems to depend on essesential being, for without it, by definition, there would be no essence from which existential being could escape. Therefore, these spheres of being appear to be mutually dependent and equally vital to the creation and maintenance of reality. However, it is existential being that provides reality with its raw presence, its manifestation, its present being. Not recognizing this fact and trying to explain the world using only essesential being is the fundamental sin of mathematical physics. The result is a purely abstract world, a world without an existing now, a world without the "ing" of being. Such a world is not our world. To assume this equivalence is merely to pretend that our models are isomorphic to the external world that they were created to explain. But this is not true. Reality is not an abstract model. Reality "is".

Consciousness is Existential Being

Beyond consciousness are there other examples of existential being? I do not know. Is consciousness just one type of existential being, the one that we are most intimately acquainted with? I do not know. For the rest of this book I will primarily use the word consciousness instead of existential being. This is being done for the sake of reducing jargon. However, keep in mind that the core thesis of this book is that the difference between essesential and existential being is fundamental to understanding the nature of reality. I would hate for the mundane words of "consciousness" and "physical" to obscure the fact that the primary difference between them is whether they exist solely within or solely beyond their essence.

Why it is Impossible for Matter/Energy to Hold on to Existential Being

At this point you may be asking whether or not elementary particles need to be isomorphic to their essence. What if we are making a mistake? What if the physical world could just as easily been comprised of existential matter? The idea of existential matter is certainly congruent with our common sense logic, as the macro physical objects that our logic is designed to deal with are functionally existential in an everyday sense. However, upon careful examination, it can be shown that a physical universe comprised of existential elementary particles is impossible, as being physical and being existential are mutually exclusive attributes.

If they were to exist, each existential elementary particle would first need to have the ability to carry its own distinguishable history. Without this initial step, they could hold on to no existence beyond their essence because their essences would be identical to others of the same type. This necessary distinguishable history would have to be carried physically. To have an elementary particle carry its physical history would mean it would have to hold subtle physical manifestations of its history, going back possibly to the time of the big bang, to make it distinguishable from others of the same type. This is difficult to conceive of, as we have no place to put the markings of a history. The standard model of particle physics suggests that elementary particles are point-like, having little or no spatial extension. Will these physical manifestations of distinguishability be bumps, scrapes, or other slight variations in mass or charge that are present in the body of an elementary particle? Does not the idea of an elementary particle imply that it cannot have such physical variations that are necessarily of an order of size less than that which is considered elementary? We can already see in this world of existential matter that the concept of an elementary particle would not be useful, as everything would have the potential for an infinite regression to smaller and smaller scales. In this hypothetical world matter would not be composed of "building blocks" but of completely unique particles, which consequently would preclude a normative chemistry as well as mathematically based descriptions of physical laws that can be generalized from one situation to another. It may appear no wonder that our current physics can be explained so well with mathematics, as essesential matter is a perfect subject for such an explanation.

Even if, in our hypothetical world, every elementary physical particle were somehow distinguishable in its mathematical description, that would not be enough for matter to gain its existential independence. It would still need to escape the essence of that mathematical description; it would have to be irreducible. If not, we would have a world full of trillions and trillions of individually novel elementary particles that remain exactly their essence. This is no different conceptually from having a handful that remain exactly their essence.

To escape their essence existential elementary particles would need to not only carry a distinguishable history, but they would need to be perpetually incomplete so they could not be described entirely by their essence, which would result in their being essesential. They would have to lack an equivalence with themselves. They would need to constantly exist as having some yet indefinable properties so their existence could never be completed. If their being ever became completed, their existence would at once equal their essence, and their being would therefore become essesential. The impossibility arises from the fact that existential elementary particles, being physical, would require a physical manifestation for all of this unlimited information regarding their essence. This would require each particle to be physically infinite, perpetually growing physical manifestations of its in-completeness to escape becoming its essence. If the information for existential matter's perpetual growth were contained in the physical particles themselves, or even in their physical neighbors, we would be right back to where we started from. They would be essesential because all of the information would be contained in the physical system. To summarize, existential elementary particles would have to be free of a specific essesential definition, while simultaneously being distinguishable physically from all others of the same type. These requirements for existential being are paradoxical when applied to matter. They cannot be simultaneously satisfied. How can an elementary particle carry within itself that which allows for an extremely specific physical manifestation of its history, and at the same time, be irreducible? The elementary particles that comprise the matter and energy of the physical universe are, and must be, essesential.

In contrast, as shown earlier, consciousness easily fits these requirements for existential being. Consciousness is not bound by the first law of thermodynamics in that, unlike elementary particles, temporal extensions of consciousness are constantly being created and destroyed. Because each temporal extension is relentlessly marched towards its own nonexistence, it remains necessarily incomplete for the entire duration of its existence. Distinguishability does not pose the same problem for consciousness as it does for elementary particles for the same reason. It is not simply because temporal extensions of consciousness exist for a fraction of a second and elementary particles can exist for billions of years. It is because consciousness is perpetually in a state of incompleteness due to its imminent nonexistence. Within the span of each temporal extension there is no distinguishability problem because two incomplete things can never equal each other. An incomplete thing cannot demonstrate any sort of exact equivalence. It can never be pinned down.

Consciousness' Limited Life Span

It is the limited life span of temporal extensions of consciousness that underpin their irreducibility. This seems to be the key to everything. Nothing else in reality perpetually faces its imminent nonexistence in such a way. Temporal extensions of consciousness are constantly being created and destroyed, and it is exactly this ceaseless state of pending destruction that frees each temporal extension from existing as its essence.

Admittedly this view of consciousness is at odds with our natural conceptualization of it. In everyday life, when I think of my consciousness, I think of it as mine, I think of it as myself, as Rick Lucido's ongoing stream of experience. In viewing consciousness as a being that is constantly being created and destroyed we seemed to have lost the ego, the "I", the personhood of consciousness. I know that we did and that doing so seems strange. However, the consciousness that has live existence beyond its essence, the consciousness that (as will be described in the next chapter) can collapse a wave function, consists only of a fraction of a second extension in time. It is not what you may think of as your personhood, your spirit, your ego, or your soul. That is not to say that these things do not exist, it is just to say that they are not part of the ontological machinery.

To further explain this we can go back to Sartre (1936) who argues that there is no ego, no "I", in consciousness. In fact consciousness is itself devoid of any property. Sartre begins by making the distinction between the pre-reflective and the reflective consciousness. The pre-reflective consciousness is the consciousness of the moment. When you look at a red apple, when you are conscious of it, you are experiencing "consciousness of apple" (its shape, color, taste etc.). There is no "I" connected to this moment, there is only consciousness of the apple or apple consciousness. If you then change your focus and begin to think about the fact you are conscious of the apple, you change to the reflective consciousness, meaning your consciousness of the apple becomes itself the object for consciousness; you are conscious of being conscious of the apple. But even then, there is still always a pre-reflective consciousness, which would have as its content not the apple in itself but your past consciousness of being conscious of the apple. It is this ever present pre-reflective consciousness that escapes essence, and this consciousness always exists without an "I". Therefore, because it is lacking an "I", the pre-reflective consciousness can be considered much more universal than we give it credit for in everyday life. This point will be important as we move forward in the next chapter and try to finally put everything together.

6

The Basic Workings of Naturalistic Idealism

So far this theory has separated reality into two profoundly different domains of being.

Essesential Being: the being of matter/energy. It has all of its existence bound up in its essence, its defining information. Its being is 100% reducible to information.

Existential Being: the being of a presently occurring temporal extension of consciousness. It has being beyond its essence precisely because it is fundamentally irreducible to information.

The challenge now is to integrate these two spheres of being into an idealistic ontology that is consistent with all the empirical facts of science. It needs to be demonstrated how a reality comprised solely of consciousness (existential being) and information (essesential being) would look exactly like the reality that we currently observe. Specifically, to be taken seriously, this idealistic ontology will have to be able to explain the following within its framework.

1. Why consciousness is necessary to collapse the wave function and how it causes the collapse to occur.

2. How causation works in the absence of objectively existing elementary particles.

3. Why causation appears to be indeterminate at a microphysical level and determined at a macro physical level.

4. How the universe worked for billions of years before consciousness and life had evolved.

Providing these explanations will require me to present a conceptualization of reality that is unfamiliar, a reality where there are no self-sustaining physical things persisting objectively in time, a reality where there is no space. In this conceptualization, reality will consist of two components that progress in time: temporal extensions of consciousness and information.

A Different View

Billions of conscious experiences are co-occurring at every instance of time: the seeing of a red truck, the not seeing of a red truck, the feeling of being punched in the face, the smell of eggs, the sound of a gunshot, the feeling of wetness, the taste of a banana, sinus pressure, the sight of a Monet, orgasm, the feeling of cold, the feeling of warmth, the taste of sugar, sharp stomach pain, seeing nothing but dark, seeing grass, feeling the onset of a sneeze, the taste of blood, hearing absolutely nothing, seeing a yellow duck coming towards you, etc. The experiences of the billions of humans on earth, along with other animals (who also may have conscious experiences), along with the potential of nonhuman consciousness in other places throughout the universe, create a constant overlapping, a rich layering, of co-occurring conscious experiences. It is imperative to remember that in a world without space these experiences cannot be thought of as occurring in separate spatial locations (i.e., people's heads). Without space there can be no location where an experience can occur. Therefore, in idealism, experiences must be thought of as being stacked up on top of each other in time, billions (at least) of co-occurring conscious experiences every instant, flashing in and out of existence in a relentless manner. Reality will thus be conceived as the entanglement of these co-occurring conscious experiences.

This relentless flow of overlapping temporal extensions of consciousness is ordered by the force of consistency in entanglement, the same force that was highlighted in the EPR experiments reviewed two chapters ago. Everything must yield to the force of consistency. Nature simply does not allow for a paradox. The primacy of this force appears to be a necessary outcome of conceptualizing matter and energy as information. This is because consistency in entanglement provides the rules that the information must adhere to. It gives the information a defined space; it holds it to within certain borders, thereby preventing it from completely decohereing into nothingness. In idealism, consistency in entanglement can be thought of as the fundamental ontological force because, by constraining the possibilities of essesential being, it supplies it with its existence.

To demonstrate this, consider the piece of paper that you are now reading from. As you read these printed words your temporal extensions of consciousness are bringing them, along with the rest of the essesential beings tied to each observation, into a consistent relationship with the history of being that brought about this current situation. From one temporal extension to the next the elementary particles comprising the paper must behave in a manner consistent with the three levels of entanglement that have bearing on this situation. These entanglements are the direct ones occurring within the same temporal extension, concurrent entanglements with other temporal extensions, and the historical entanglements that have given rise to the current situation in which the temporal extension of consciousness is occurring. For the purpose of clarity, each level will be explained separately. However, in reality, entanglement is best understood as a unitary structure.

Consistency of essesential being within a temporal extension of consciousness is the most straight forward level of entanglement. The word being read on the paper cannot both be what it is and at the same time be something else. To be so would be an inconsistency that could not exist within the indivisible unity of being that is a temporal extension. Therefore, essesential being in a temporal extension must have a certain measure of specificity regarding its essence. That specificity, constrained by what has come before, will constrain all that comes after. However, more than just the words on the page are entangled in this situation. For example, the essesential particles in the light that allows you to see the words, the lamp that is the light source, and the power lines all the way to the power station are all directly entangled within the temporal extension of consciousness. You could even go further and include the fossil fuels being burned to produce the power and their creation millions of years ago. All of these macro essesential beings necessary for this grand chain to occur have gained a consistent existence as their specific essence.

However, this chain of consistency involving only one temporal extension has limits. From the perspective of only the single direct entanglement questions regarding the average age of the employees working at the power company that day and how far your trees have overgrown can have many different answers. The answers to these questions can be almost anything. They are only limited by the force of consistency to the point at which they would make the direct entanglements of reading by the lamp light impossible, such as no one is at the power company or my trees are interfering with the power lines. Fortunately, reality does not allow for such gross ambiguities, as entanglements are at work on two other levels.

Concurrent entanglements with other temporal extensions of consciousness also constrain essesential being. Using our previous example, the person working at the power company, in his temporal extensions of consciousness, is also part of the web of consistency, as is the person taking a walk outside observing that your trees are not interfering with the power lines. What they observe must fit with what you observe in reading by the lamp. In other words, the essesential beings existing in a temporal extension of consciousness must be consistent with every other concurrent temporal extension of consciousness; all points of observation must hold an equally valid perspective on reality.

Lastly, historical entanglements bring about the physical law with which essesential beings must be consistent. Consistency must be shown in between direct entanglements occurring in sequential temporal extensions. The paper in your hands cannot simply fail to exist during the temporal extension following one where it did exist. That would violate thermodynamics and Newton's laws. These laws have power due to their historical embedding in the web of consistency. In so far as the essesential being in a previous temporal extension is consistent with such laws as those in classical physics, that consistency must be continued in subsequent extensions. These laws are carried forward in time by the force of consistency in temporal extensions of consciousness. They are not a result of the particular nature of essesential beings, for they have no being over time with which to carry the laws that would be necessitated by their nature. To illustrate this, consider a room with only one door and no windows, having no other connections to the outside world. A person looks inside and sees that there is a chair in the center of the room. She leaves the room and stands in front of the door to be sure that no one else enters. She then enters the room five minutes later to find the chair in the same spot. The laws of classical physics held, obviously, for the state of the chair in the room even though it was not in a direct entanglement. The laws of classical physics that the room must show consistency with were being carried in the temporal extensions of consciousness of the person in-between the observations of the room. Her being between measurements of the state of the room was connected to the rest of existence in a multitude of entanglements, each reaffirming classical physics by their prior state. Therefore the state of the room by the second observation was compelled to demonstrate consistency with the totality of entanglements that her temporal extension of consciousness brought to bear at the point of observation[10].

---

[10] The central shortcoming in Berkley's idealism (that it requires God to constantly be observing all of creation so that objects can exists when no

Why Consciousness is Necessary to Collapse the Wave Function and How it Causes the Collapse to Occur

Temporal extensions of consciousness collapse the wave function by connecting it to the web of consistency. The superposition ends when a choice is forced upon nature in order to satisfy the requirement for consistency in entanglement. That, simply stated, is the answer.

The conceptual difficulties posed by entanglement and non-locality are only problems when matter is falsely assumed to independently persist in time. If we are working off of the materialist perspective then it seems absurd that observation should be able to apply any force to objectively existing elementary particles. It should not be able to force nature to make a choice. However, when matter is viewed as information, wave function collapse upon observation becomes an obvious necessity. Remember that information, for it to exist as information, requires specificity. It requires constraint. It cannot exist independently without stretching itself out into nonexistence. The superposition, the uncollapsed wave function, is an example of information living on its own. It is literally nothing. However, when an observation occurs, the experimenter's temporal extension of consciousness forces it to become something by compelling it to manifest a degree of specificity regarding itself (e.g., spin, momentum, position) that would demonstrate congruence with the rest of the web of consistency. This is the collapse of the wave function.

---

one else is perceiving them) can be resolved by the application of the concept of consistency in entanglement.

How Causation Works in the Absence of Objectively Existing Elementary Particles

In materialism causation works through a mechanistic force, whereas in idealism causation must work through a teleological force. In the materialist worldview, mechanistic causation results from local interactions of things in themselves. Causation is not based on rule following but on the interactions between the intrinsic nature of particles themselves. A good metaphor for mechanistic causation would be to consider it as a "push force". Picture in your mind someone pushing a car. Notice how that push force is not end based. The force is behind the object. Once the force is applied what actually happens to the car, how far it rolls, and what it runs into have nothing further to do with the causal agent. Mechanistic causation is the everyday conceptualization of causation and the causal conceptualization of classical physics. If we consider physical objects to have an objective persistence through time it is indeed the only type of causation that is even conceivable. However, you might be asking yourself how can mechanistic causation work with matter existing as information? The answer is that it cannot. A "2" cannot run into a "3" and force it to become "5". Mechanistic causation of this type is completely incompatible with idealism.

The opposite of mechanistic causation is teleological causation, or end based causation. In teleological causation the outcome of a causal event is not determined by the intrinsic properties of interacting objects, but of the rules resulting from the force of consistency in entanglement. For example, in experimental tests of the EPR paradox the measurement of the second particle is teleologically forced to show consistency with the previous measurement of the first particle. It has to be consistent. This need for consistency is the fundamental force that determines all causal outcomes. This of course is easy to see in experiments with entangled particles. However, the same process is at work with more mundane cases of causation. The trick is to see that what appears to be acts mechanistic causation can also be understood as instances of teleological causation. For example, remember that person pushing the car. We can contend that there is not an objectively existing car and that there is not an objectively existing body that is pushing it and we still get an outcome that is consistent with the laws of physics. Gravity and electromagnetism are still at work in determining what is going to happen (e.g., how far the car is going to roll), but their power over the events can just as easily be conceptualized as mathematical mandates that the outcome must lie within. It just depends how you view it.

Why Causation Appears to be Indeterminate at a Microphysical Level and Determined at a Macro Physical Level

If the primary causal force in reality is that of teleological consistency, then micro indeterminacy moving to macro determinism is the necessary outcome. This is because the force of consistency is not conceptually mandated to exist on all levels the way that the traditional "push forces" of physics are. The force of consistency has a floor, beneath which it has no power. For example, consider as before the paper that you are now reading. The essesential beings in your temporal extensions of consciousness must demon-strate consistency with the three levels of entanglement as shown earlier. However, every specific detail not in a type of entanglement exists as a non-being underneath the power of the force of consistency to confer it with an exact existence in our world. If an electron in the paper could have a different position or momentum here or there that would not have a macro effect on the levels of entanglement, then that electron has no specific existence as its essence. It has rather a constrained essesential existence. Its existence as its essence is spread out over a set of all the possibilities (Schrödinger's wave function) that are congruent with the entanglements with which it must show consistency. This probability distribution represents the general pattern of results needed over time to show consistency with the entanglements having bearing on the situation. Below the force of consistency there is literally nothing to require the essesential being to be exactly this or that. The point where it does not matter what outcome is needed to make consistency work is the point at which reality's chief ontological and causal force runs out of power. It has the means to force an outcome but not the means to specify it exactly. Meaning, when we measure details of a particle not previously regulated by consistency to a measure of specificity, we need to get a result (the collapse of the wave function). When we measure, there needs to be a particle there whose state would be congruent with consistency. If there was no such particle, that would result in an inconsistency with the macro entanglements, which would be impossible. However, the state of these essesential particles (being information) is determined solely by the need for consistency, not by their previous state, position, momentum, and so on. The controlled randomness of quantum mechanics follows directly from this. There is a causal force, but that force is a force of constraint not one of exertion. Conceptualizing the force of consistency in such a way allows us to explain random fluctuations at the micro physical level while holding on to determined physical causation at the macro physical level. The classical/quantum border becomes the point at which consistency loses its power to specify essence.

How the Universe Worked for Billions of Years before Consciousness and Life Evolved

What about the history of the universe? What about evolution? How could a metaphysical framework rely on consciousness when it took billions of years for consciousness to evolve? What was happening before consciousness existed? Was anything happening before consciousness existed?

While I am certainly not a creationist, I do think that reality (or at the very least this reality/universe) had a moment of inception. There was a beginning. The question I would like to address here is how this beginning would look in naturalistic idealism as compared to materialism. In materialism, things are straightforward. First, the big bang and inflation occurred. This was the event that created the matter/energy and space of the physical universe that has objectively existed in time for the last thirteen billion plus years. After this event the universe cooled. Gravity got to work and gasses condensed and formed stars. Within the cores of these stars heavy elements were produced under immense heat and pressure. These stars eventually used up all of their fuel and exploded in colossal supernova, expelling the heavy elements into space. About 4.5 billion years

ago our sun was formed, and materials from past supernova explosions formed the iron core of our planet. The
earth absorbed a constant barrage of asteroids for millions
of years. Around 4 billion years ago oceans formed. In
these oceans through yet some poorly understood conver-
gence of events some of the molecules started to self-rep-
licate. Over millions of years they evolved into complex
single celled life. The earth continued to cool. Complex
single celled life evolved into complex multi celled life.
This life left the ocean and learned to thrive on the land
and in the air. At some unknown point one of these multi-
celled creatures, after reaching some critical point in brain
complexity, became conscious. More time passed. Modern humans evolved. They took up farming and built cit-
ies. Sometime later you and I were born and now here we
are.

In this materialist timeline of events the advent of life
and consciousness are simply footnotes to a much longer
progression. These events occurred irrespective of consciousness. They are considered to be the result of the
presence of objective phenomenon brutely persisting
through time on their own power. In contrast, within the
framework of naturalistic idealism the first temporal extension of conscious experience plays a much more important
role, for it would have brought about the collapse of the
first universal wave function. Let me explain.

In the beginning let us assume that there was nothing;
there was only information without any measure of specificity to it. Let us view it as a gigantic uncollapsed wave
function. This wave function was unlike anything that
might be manifested in a modern physics experiment. The
untold trillions of collapses that have occurred throughout

time have tightened the web of consistency to a point where there is significant constraint on the outcomes of future measurements. This constraint (most likely) continues to grow as collapses occur resulting in less wiggle room within the web of consistency. However, things looked much different at the inception of the universe. There was, presumably, no consciousness, and therefore no wave function collapse. The possibilities for the state of the early universe (being that it is only information) are completely unrestrained; they are not bound to show consistency with anything. It is a blank canvas with all possibilities simultaneously existing. Such as the possibility that the initial conditions were such that the big bang stalled shortly after starting and inflation never took place, or that inflation occurred too rapidly before gravity had a chance to operate. In these scenarios life and consciousness never evolve. However, both of these possibilities are existing in the first wave function, along with the possibility that the big bang occurred exactly as we have record of it and the preconditions were set for our existence. Of these many possibilities, only one had occurred, the one that allowed for consciousness to exist. This is exactly as should be expected. Any possible scenario that would have ruled out life and consciousness from evolving would never be able to manifest itself precisely because there would be nothing to collapse the initial wave function. Thus from the perspective of this idealism, the only way that the history of the universe could have played out is with a scenario that would ultimately lead to the first temporal extension of consciousness. This first temporal extension would have collapsed the first wave function thereby locking in the history that would have been consistent with the formation of stars and galaxies, one that would have given rise to a planet such as the earth with an atmosphere and liquid water, the history that would have held the nearly impossible accident of self-replicating structures (life) that would evolve over millions of years to produce the first temporal extension of consciousness. This history that had once existed only as a potential option in an infinite sea of possibilities became actualized as a fact. The record of everything that occurred in the past on the particular road to this moment is preserved just as if it would have had objective existence the whole time.

This idea of a universal wave function collapsing upon the arrival of consciousness is not mine, and it is not new. Using vastly different terminology, of course, it goes back at least until the time of the 19th century to the idealistic philosopher Arthur Schopenhauer who writes:

> "On the other hand, the law of causality and the treatment and investigation of nature which is based upon it, lead us necessarily to the conclusion that, in time, each more highly organized state of matter has succeeded a cruder state: so that the lower animals existed before men, fishes before land animals, plants before fishes, and the unorganized before all that is organized; that, consequently, the original mass had to pass through a long series of changes before the first eye could be opened. And yet, the existence of this whole world remains ever dependent upon the first eye that opened, even if it were that of an insect. For such an eye is a necessary condition of the possibility of knowledge, and the whole world exists only in and

for knowledge, and without it is not even thinkable. The world is entirely idea, and as such demands the knowing subject as the supporter of its existence."

Idealism Solves the Problem of Fine Tuning

The best part of this idealistic conceptualization of history is that we get the added bonus of explaining the problem of the Fine Tuning of the universe. Over the last several decades physicists have increasingly identified how amazingly fine-tuned our universe is to support our existence. I will limit myself here to just two quick examples. First, if the strength of the force that binds particles together in atomic nuclei were only a thousandth of a unit weaker, only hydrogen could exist. If it were a thousandth of a unit stronger then no hydrogen would exist as it would have been fused up shortly after the big bang. In either scenario we are left with a universe without planets and stars, a universe without life and consciousness. Secondly, the overall density of the universe also seems to be extremely fined tuned. At its inception, if the density of the universe would have been just one part in 10^{15} (i.e., 0.0000000000001%) larger or smaller then the universe would have either collapsed on itself or expanded so fast that gravity would not have been able to pull materials together to form stars and galaxies. Likewise slight changes to either the gravitational force, the speed of light, or the electromagnetic force would have produced a universe inhospitable to life. These constants all seem to be fined tuned to produce a universe with the structures and conditions necessary for complex objects and life to form.

Out of a near infinite number of possibilities we find ourselves in a universe that has the mathematical properties necessary for atoms, molecules, stars, and planets to form, a universe that has set the preconditions for life. How can materialists explain this fine tuning with a cosmology that does not select for it in the way that idealism does? Many physicists resort to the concept of the multiverse to explain this. The multiverse is the contention that there actually exists a near infinite, or an actual infinite, number of different universes other than our own. Each universe has properties that may be vastly different than our own, most of which would not contain the properties that would allow for any structures to form, let alone life. They contend that in these universes there is obviously no one there to observe. There only exist observers in the universes that are fine tuned in such a way to have observers. Therefore, using the anthropic principal, even if the odds are a hundred trillion to one that a particular universe could exist that would be able to support sentient life, we should not be surprised that we find ourselves in that very universe. From a materialist perspective, the concept of the multiverse makes the problem of fine tuning go away.

Now to be fair, the concept of the multiverse is complex and multifaceted, there are different types, some of it of it supported by the concept of inflation. So I am not arguing that the concept of a multiverse is not useful, and that there is not good reason to consider that some of it may be true. What I am saying is that explaining why our universe is so amazingly fined tuned for our existence by asserting that every universe that can exist does exist is a cop out. However, for materialist it is an absolute necessity. Without it they are utterly stuck. They have no other way to explain fine tuning [11]. Idealism, in contrast, does.

This is not an Idealism of Individual Souls

I would like to emphatically clarify that this theory is not an idealism of individual souls. I am not arguing that reality consists of individual psychic entities. Instead the idealism presented here is an idealism of billions (at least) of indivisible moments of conscious experience. The idea of personhood, while vitally important to us in other ways, plays no part in the fundamental ontological machinery. It is an abstraction that comes later.

Remember that in the last chapter it was discussed that there is no "I" in the pre reflective consciousness. Philosophically speaking, to say that "I am conscious of the apple" is not technically accurate. What I should say is that consciousness of a red apple is existing. (It is very difficult to write about this and not get tripped up over words, as our language tends to put personhood into everything. So I beg the reader to forgive some conceptual imperfections while I attempt to address this using plain language). If Sartre was correct in his analysis that consciousness is itself devoid of intrinsic content, and that it manifests itself only as the experience of something else, then there should be no difference between Rick Lucido's red, the Queen of England's red, or you the reader's red. There is only consciousness of red. These adjectives marking the possession of the red (e.g., Rick Lucido's, the Queen of England's) are

---

[11] The only other way to explain fine tuning, besides calling it an incredible coincidence, is to evoke the idea of divine creation. Many theists have used the fine tuning of the universe as an argument for the existence of god.

merely tangential. These adjectives exist only in the reflective consciousness, where there exists consciousness of a past conscious experience of red. In this scenario of course the red is possessed by someone. But this is not "red consciousness". It is reflective consciousness; it is consciousness of being conscious, or more accurately consciousness of past consciousness. But as was mentioned earlier, even here there still exists a pre-reflective consciousness, that which is the consciousness of the ego (not that of the red). Therefore, this ever present pre-reflective consciousness manifests only as its contents (e.g., red, cold, square, C#m.). Thus, this pre-reflective consciousness is by its nature universal. It is possessed by no one. It is not yours or mine. It just is.

I realize that I may be sounding like a Buddhist here by contending that the self is an illusion and consciousness is universal. I am not denying this. This is not a religious book, so I will go no further here on this point other than to briefly acknowledge that the idealism that I am advocating is consistent in many ways with certain Buddhist metaphysics, and, intellectually speaking, it would be disingenuous to not acknowledge that I am in its debt.

A Simple Metaphor

To summarize the preceding, we can say reality does not consist of a universe extended in space but of consciousness interacting with information that is constrained by the force of consistency. This is very hard to picture in one's mind. Without space you cannot expect to stand back and see the big picture. There would be nothing to see. Therefore, any type of visual representation of this idealism would be conceptually dubious and misleading. However, people, especially people like me, sometimes need a visual metaphor to hold on to, some picture to place in their mind. In ending this chapter, I am going to take a chance and offer one. If a metaphor must be made I think that I would offer the following imperfect one:

> Picture reality as an infinitesimal speck of white silence where billions of experiences flash in and out of existence, bound and ordered by unbreakable rules that have emerged from the force of consistency, rules that were once known as the physical world. Looking at it from the outside it contains nothing; it is nothing. Only from the interior can it been seen that our spaceless speck is in fact, for us, everything.

7

Mental Causation

"A man who wills commands something within himself
that renders obedience, or that he believes renders
obedience"

-- Friedrich Nietzsche, *Beyond Good and Evil*

Mental causation is not a problem for materialists. If one
believes that conscious experience is ontologically equivalent to neurophysiological events (i.e., matter in motion)
then the question of how consciousness can affect the
brain is already answered. Consciousness is the brain. It
is all physical. No explanatory problem exists. However,
for dualists, who believe both in the fundamentality of consciousness and physical realism, mental causation poses a
significant explanatory problem. If conscious thoughts
and emotions are going to have any effect on human behavior they must affect the physical brain physically, but
how could consciousness, something that is completely
nonphysical, ever have an effect on objectively existing
matter? How could something nonphysical push something physical, physically? This has historically been the
most difficult problem for dualism. It is what fueled Gilbert Ryle's original epigrams about the "ghost in the machine". Idealist thinkers, however, have generally remained
silent on the issue. I think that this silence is a mistake.
Idealists cannot be content to simply contend that since

everything is ultimately mental there is no explanatory problem. This is not good enough. Clarification is required. While determining how consciousness could influence information is admittedly much easier than explaining how it could influence objectively existing material objects (i.e., nerve cells), this mechanism of influence still needs to be explained. Idealism needs to provide its own answers from its own perspective. This will be the task of the current chapter.

In naturalistic idealism the division lines between ourselves and external reality are nontraditional. In my everyday thinking my consciousness, my brain, and my body are thought of as being *me* and the room I am in and the furniture on which I sit are considered to be external to me. The division line is placed between the biological and the non biological. However, in naturalistic idealism your brain and your body, just like the room you are in and the furniture on which you sit, are essesential objects: they exist as information. The division line is not placed at the biological boundary, but rather it is placed at the boundary between consciousness and essesential objects. Your neuro-biological state is part of the wave function, information that must conform to the demands of consistency in entanglement. It is simply the last step. When I see a red apple, the apple, the light that travels from it to my eyes, my eyes themselves, and the pattern of activation in the occipital lobe of my brain all exist as part of the wave function that collapses upon the occurrence of the temporal extension of consciousness that witnesses it.

Dualist's theories of mental causation typically rely on consciousness' role in the collapse of the wave function to bridge the gap between mind and matter. A central problem with these theories is that they fail to translate well to our everyday macro level consciousness, which does not directly observe neural functioning in the same way that a physicist may observe quantum phenomena by looking at an instrument. For example, the theoretical physicist Henry Stapp (2005) provides a model where the efficacy of consciousness arises from the Quantum Zeno Effect; rapidly successive measurements on a quantum system stop it from evolving and effectively restrict the system to the state in which it was initially measured. He contends that focused attention through mental effort can actualize potential brain states through such rapid continued measurement. In neuroscience, Friedrich Beck and John Eccles (1992) proposed a model of nonphysical causation that relies on exocytosis, the process by which neurotransmitters are expelled into the synaptic cleft (how neurons communicate with each other). They argue that this process is probabilistic and quantum mechanical. In their model, conscious intention can momentarily increase the probability for exocytosis in selected cortical areas, thereby causing a physical effect. Finally, the physicist Evan Harris Walker (1998) proposed a model whereby a global system of electron tunneling in the brain provides the vehicle for the efficacy of consciousness. This model, like its predecessors, is also based on consciousness directly effecting the collapse of the wave function.

While these models demonstrate the potential for quantum indeterminacy to affect brain behavior, they fail to provide a plausible mechanism for the efficacy of consciousness. These causal models are unsatisfying because they require our consciousness to be aware of the functioning of billions of microscopic interactions at time intervals that we cannot consciously process. In reality, our everyday consciousness only seems to be observing macro events that occur in macro time, not neural functioning. Since it is our daily conscious awareness for which we seek a mechanism of efficacy, theorists must be careful not to fall into a trap of inadvertently giving it omnipotence. Our consciousness is literally what we are aware of. That is it. For this reason, mechanisms of mental causation that rely on consciousness directly influencing state selection at the time of the collapse of the wave function are fatally flawed. A workable mechanism of mental causation must allow consciousness to retain its macro limitations.

The Act of Willing and the Temporality of Consciousness

By self-examination consider what happens in consciousness when you decide to move your finger. After doing so ask yourself this question. In your mind, are you consciously willing the particular sequence of synaptic transmissions necessary to send an electrical signal down to the muscles in your hand? I would think not. When we will an action, all we are actually doing is conceiving of the final macro outcome, such as the movement of the finger. It feels as though our consciousness is giving an order to our body, which faithfully complies, although in our consciousness we are unaware of the physical steps that the brain and body must complete to execute the order. This point is critical. Any proposed mechanism of mental causation must work in a way that is consistent with the limits of our conscious awareness. Consciously, we do not will the first neuron to fire; what we will is the final movement of the finger. It is important to consider what it means to will an action if one is only willing the outcome of the action as opposed to the initial step needed to produce it. It is as if our will operates not as a "first cause," which through some yet unknown physical force knocks down the initial neural domino that leads to the desired behavior, but as an executive sending an order to his employees which states that all work for the week is to be completed by Friday. The cause for the work's completion is the executive order. The executive's order, or his will, has power because the employees are bound to obey it, not because he has harnessed the power of one of the physical forces to make the employees legs move. The causal power flows from the nature of the relationship between the executive and the workers. The workers have to obey. They have to make the state of the factory consistent with the order. The causal force is therefore teleological rather than mechanistic.

It also needs to be considered that in consciousness the willing of an action and the observation of that willed fulfilled occur simultaneously. You will your finger to move and you watch it move. There is no time lapse. They are both occurring within the same temporal extension of consciousness. If you are currently watching your still finger, it is because you have not yet willed it to move; in the same conscious instant you eventually do, you will observe it moving. Try yourself to notice a time lag between the moment of will and that of observation. If you cannot notice it, then by definition, they occur simultaneously in consciousness. In contrast, these events obviously do not co-occur in the physical domain. A sequence of neurons fire in your brain, eventually sending out signals to the muscles that contract to move your finger. After that, signals from the nerves in your finger and from your eyes travel back to your brain where they are interpreted as the observation of the action of finger movement. All this takes time. In the physical domain there is a time gap between the moment of will and the moment of the observation of that will fulfilled, but in the domain of consciousness there is not.

Apart from helping it to escape its essence as was discussed in chapter five, the temporally extended nature of consciousness also provides a means to explain its efficacy. Consider an indivisible temporal extension of willed consciousness spread out over a period of physical time. Where in that chunk of conscious time can we locate the physical present? Where is the past, the future? In our temporally extended consciousness these notions of time have no existence; all points within the temporal extension, i.e., the moment of will and the observation of that will fulfilled, are experienced as occurring simultaneously. In other words, the present, the immediate past, and the immediate future in physical time all exist within the duration of the life span of each indivisible temporal extension of willed consciousness.

Temporal Extensions of Willed Consciousness

From the perspective of physical time, a temporal extension of willed consciousness begins with a will moment, which can be defined as the start of neural activity related to enacting the willed behavior, and ends with the observation moment, the interpretation of the afferent signals related to the willed behavior. Since these two moments occur simultaneously in consciousness, at the first physical instant of a temporal extension of consciousness the conscious observation of the will fulfilled gains a future metaphysical existence. At this time, from the perspective of the physical, the observation of the will fulfilled becomes an imminent certainty with which it must contend. Everything in neuroscience suggests that the neural state at the end of a temporal extension of consciousness would need to be consistent with the conscious observation of the will fulfilled, and it is. People do not usually experience themselves moving their arms when in fact they are still. Thousands of times each day our consciousness puts forth executive orders in to the immediate future, and the brain evolves into a state that shows consistency with that observation by the end of the temporal extension of consciousness.

Nature may achieve this consistency by influencing the quantum indeterminacy in exocytosis, as per the model of Beck and Eccles, by the electron tunneling mechanism suggested by Walker, or by some other neural process affected by quantum indeterminacy that may lead to macro changes in brain states. However, the mechanism by which consciousness can influence this indeterminacy is a consequence of the brain's entanglement with the experiential future, not on consciousness' initiation of the collapse of the wave function as often argued. This mechanism of conscious efficacy is advantageous in that all it requires of consciousness is to make global observations of its macro state, which is all it can actually do. In doing so, it provides the necessary behavioral end, the executive order that demands compliance. Everything else falls into place automatically as per the force of nature's need for consistency. Consciousness is entangled with the brain. The divergent nature of temporality within this entanglement allows for consciousness to observe its will first, thereby forcing the brain to catch up and demonstrate consistency.

Consider the implications of this proposed mechanism in regards to how the relationship between consciousness and neural states evolve over time. Willed behaviors do not come out of nowhere. They are the result of conscious processing evolving over time eventually leading up to the moment of will. The neural state follows consciousness closely on this path, as consistency must be demonstrated after each temporal extension. Therefore, the neural state at the start of the temporal extension that may initiate a willed behavior should be very close to enacting that behavior by itself, through the means of physically determined processes. Consciousness has driven the state of the brain to that point and then proceeds to give it a final pull in the direction projected by the observation of the will fulfilled. Therefore, as we can see, consciousness would never shock the brain with demands for consistency that the brain is not prepared for, because they are never more than one temporal extension of consciousness (a fraction of a second) away from total consistency. However, even though the neural state is always prepared for the next temporal extension, there are times when the behavior cannot be enacted for other reasons. For example, a musician playing a new piece of music attempts to will a novel and difficult pattern of finger movements. She fails to execute as she had envisioned. The conscious order has gone through and the attempt had been made, but the attempt was experienced as a failure. This may have been because there was not enough space in the indeterminacy available to produce the willed behavior as she had envisioned. The brain had not yet set up the behavior through well-worn neural pathways. Too much adjustment was required to get to the desired result. In this way, the current mechanism fits well with the everyday notions of the limits of our will, namely that it is easier to perform well-practiced behaviors than novel ones.

Human Individuality of Will

Do humans have free will? I surely do not know. Taking the overall state of the philosophy of mind literature it appears to certainly be a long shot at best. Of course this consensus rests upon a materialist metaphysics, which by its very nature denies the independent existence of a consciousness that could even have the capacity for free action. However, considering the free will question from a perspective other than materialism leaves the possibility wide open. From a non materialist perspective there exist several solid arguments for free will (e.g., Bergson, 1910; Hodgson, 2005; Sartre, 1953). However, I do not want to dive any further into this complex debate, or to take sides. Instead, I would like to address how free will would look, if it were to exist, in naturalistic idealism. Within this framework the concept of free will is forced to manifest itself in an unfamiliar form. This change in perspective regarding the question of free will seems interesting to me regardless of whether or not it actually exists.

In traditional dualism conscious minds are individualized. Any type of free will that your consciousness could possess would be individualized to you. It is "your" free will. It is connected to the biological organism that is "you", that exists inside "your" head. As previously mentioned, in dualism, the division line between self and non self rests at the biological to non biological boundary. However, things are different in naturalistic idealism; consciousness is seen as being much more universal. As discussed earlier, because there is no space, conscious experiences cannot be thought to exist in particular places (i.e., people's heads) but need to be conceptualized as being stacked up on top of each other in time. This lack of separation between conscious experiences inherent in idealism requires a reconceptualization of the relationship between free will and individuality.

Psychologically our personalities, our reinforcement histories, and the immediate context of our environment determine our actions. Our personalities and our reinforcement histories are the result of complex multidirectional interactions between our genes and external influences (e.g., parenting, schooling, friends etc..). These processes are mainly deterministic and subconscious. However, as proponents of free will contend, these deterministic influences can yield to consciousness. A free consciousness can control our actions, maybe not most of the time, but hopefully when it is most important to do so. In contrast to the perspective of classical dualism, this consciousness that has the ability to override the system is not individualized to you. In naturalistic idealism everything that is individualized to you is completely determined (e.g., personality, reinforcement history, context). The part that is free (consciousness) is non-individualized. Remember that these individualized and determined behavioral tendencies are comprised of essesential being. Your brain, like every other material object, exists as information, the specifics of that information being held together and determined by the force of consistency in entanglement. Consciousness exists outside of that chain of determination because each temporal extension of consciousness literally precedes the completion of its correlate essence. But since temporal extensions of consciousness do not possess an "I", since, as Sartre argued, there is no ego in pre-reflective consciousness, then that freedom does not belong to "you"; rather it belongs to consciousness itself. In other words, from the perspective of this idealism, it seems that your individuality is determined while your freedom is universal.

For demonstration purposes allow me to hold out myself as an example. There is a 220 pound biological mass named Richard Lucido. He was born in 1977 in the midwestern United States. He attended Catholic schools for 13 years before going to college. His parents were kind and loving people. He was generally spoiled with material possessions and attention, but was also taught the value of hard work. He has predisposition to hyperactivity and excessive moodiness. On his worst days he can present as grouchy and even self-absorbed. He transitioned into adulthood during a time of peace and prosperity in his country. His childhood was spared from any significant psychological trauma. Based on these facts and thousands of others, as well as his genetic makeup (which cannot yet be so easily described), there are individual characteristics that can be ascribed to the biological entity that we can label as Richard Lucido. These resulting psychological traits are completely determined; free will has nothing to do with any of it. However, there is a universal consciousness that, being irreducible to information, and slightly ahead of physical time due to its temporally extended nature, has been directing, at times, the behavior of this Richard Lucido (along with every other sentient biological entity). However, this universal consciousness was not shaped by the biological individuality of Richard Lucido. It is not his. The same can be said for everybody. Thus naturalistic idealism appears to lead us into unfamiliar territory on the free will question. A strong libertarian free will appears to be a definite possibility, but it is a free will without individual ownership. It is a strange position indeed. I am still not sure what to make of it. In my opinion, it is the most peculiar conclusion of this entire theory.

To summarize: in naturalistic idealism each temporal extension of consciousness is presented with the determined predispositions of the biological person with which it is connected. However, because the content of the temporal extension is projected into the immediate future it is not completely bound by those determined predispositions. It is free. But since it is free and not completely determined by an individual's characteristics it therefore cannot be considered the product of that biological entity. It is therefore universal. I like to think that each temporal extension represents an original appraisal of a particular biological and situational context (which are in themselves a collection of information). The free decisions that we make do not stem from anyone's individuality, but are the product of the consciousness that we are and that animates all of reality.

8

Speculations on an Idealistic Cosmology

Why did the universe begin? What happened before the universe started to make it begin? Why is there something rather than nothing? Religion and mythology have dominated the discussion on these questions for thousands of years. In contrast, science and philosophy have yet to provide satisfying answers from within their perspectives. Regrettably, this situation may be impossible to remedy. These questions may simply be too big for the tools we currently possess. Therefore, it needs to be acknowledged that you are unlikely to find the cosmological speculations in this chapter completely satisfying. Regardless of this, I am going to present what I think to be one possible idealistic explanation for the origin of the universe. The point of presenting this is simply to demonstrate that it is possible to do so. It will, of course, have many of the same problems as any other explanation (materialistic or otherwise). My aims therefore are modest. I only endeavor to show that naturalistic idealism can produce an account that is in many ways just as good and just as bad as explanations from other perspectives.

How Do You Get Something from Nothing?

It is impossible to get something from nothing. This self evident truth seems to put up an impassable road block right at the start of any endeavor to explain the origin of reality. The way that the cosmology of materialism gets around this road block is by suggesting that although the inception of our physical universe was the big bang this was not actually the start of "everything". They postulate that there were things in existence before the big bang, such as quantum Higgs fluctuations or gigantic universe creating membranes. In these scenarios something is never really created out of nothing. They do not explain how the membranes got there, or why there should be quantum fluctuations in the first place. The explanation, if one is given, is always directed at how our universe arose from some preexisting state. In an idealistic cosmology, because everything is flipped around, we are compelled to use a different strategy. Doing so will allow us to circumvent the intractable problem of creating something from nothing, without merely avoiding it as do the materialists.

To begin, we must reconsider how we are implicitly conceptualizing the nature of, and the difference between, "something" and "nothing". What do we mean by these words? Decades of psychological research instructs us that our abstract concepts are largely metaphorical (e.g., Lakoff & Johnson, 1999). Such researchers have argued that abstract reasoning originates from the use of analogy and that philosophical and scientific inquiry are both limited and liberated by the skillful application of analogy. Therefore, it is imperative to understand the analogy that is, and has always been, implicit in the question: why is there something rather than nothing. If throughout history the question has been intractable we must consider the possibility that the analogies we have been using are simply wrong. Doing so will require us to first identify the implicit analogy commonly employed when we talk about "something" and "nothing".

Elementary mathematical training, the kind one would receive in primary school, has provided most people with basic numerical concepts. Embedded in these concepts are the implicit numerical analogies for the words "something" and "nothing". Specifically zero is "nothing" while any positive real number is "something". Unfortunately, it appears that this analogy leads to a dead end in terms of our question. You simply cannot get something from nothing, a "1" from a "0". Without the ability to produce something from nothing, as mentioned earlier, our questioning is over before it has begun. However, what if the analogy were to change? What if we were to derive new mathematical analogies for "something" and "nothing"?

Consistent with the ontology so far presented, let us posit that the correct analogy is for "nothing" to be represented by the infinite set while "something" is to be represented by any set which is not equal to the infinite set[12]. In earlier chapters we discussed the isomorphic nature of elementary particles to information. Remember what information actually is. Information is specificity, limitations on possibilities. To illustrate, if you ask someone for their name and they respond with the infinite set of every possible combination of phonemes going on forever, then they have given you "nothing". You asked for specificity and they gave you infinity. In a world where matter is isomor-

---

[12] There are many different sets of infinite numbers. For example there are an infinite amount of fractions between the numbers 1 and 2, just as there are an infinite number of positive whole numbers. When I say the infinite set, what I mean is literally everything. Nothing would be excluded. So to picture it mathematically would mean every number of every type in every direction. In other words: "boundless".

phic to information, "1" and "0" cannot signify "something" and "nothing", because "1" and "0" are both something; they are both pieces of specific information. However, infinity (the totality of everything that could ever be) is the opposite of information. It is the opposite of essential being. It therefore seems to be the perfect way to represent nothing within this idealistic framework.

Utilizing these revised analogies, the pre universe state, the original nothingness from which reality may have sprung can be conceptualized as a primordial infinity of information that contains every possible bit of information in every possible form. This primordial infinity can be conceived of as the ultimate example of information existing on its own, in that it has completely spread itself out into nonexistence. Given this, the question then becomes whether or not this hypothesized primordial infinity would be stable. Would it be possible for it to persist without specificity entering the picture? I do not think that it would be. The reason is straightforward. This primordial infinity would be immediately compelled to draw out a meta axiom related to itself. This meta axiom would hold a special level of truth that the bits of information in the infinite set do not have, that they cannot have. We can term this the axiom of incongruence and it can be simply stated as such: *the infinite set contains information statements that are incongruent with each other.* See the chart for a visual depiction.

A Small Sample of Incongruent Information Statements from an Infinite Set of Possibilities

There are 10^{78} total particles in existence	There are 10^{23} total particles in existence	There are 17 particles in existence	There are 4 particles in existence	No particles exist
There is no life in the universe	There are 10^{21} carbon based plant organisms	There exists two dragons	Only bacteria exists	Only artificial life exits
$E=mc^2$	$E=mc^{39}$	There is no energy	There is no mass	Mass and energy are not related
Strings exist and they all vibrate in 45 spatial dimensions	Strings exist and they all vibrate in 19 spatial dimensions	Strings exist and they all vibrate in 11 spatial dimensions	Strings exist and they all vibrate in 2 spatial dimensions	There are no strings
The mass of an Up Quark is 142.4 MeV/c^2	The mass of an Up Quark is 7.1 MeV/c^2	The mass of an Up Quark is 2.4 MeV/c^2	The mass of an Up Quark is 0.00001 MeV/c2	There are no Up Quarks
X=1	X=2	X=3	X=4	X=99

The preceding chart is comprised of only 30 information statements for convenience, but there is nothing theoretically stopping us from filling it up with an infinite number of squares to match the infinite number of possible information statements. In an infinite number of squares it is impossible to escape this incongruence. It is a self-evident truth that must arise from nothingness conceptualized as the infinite set. However, I would contend that the axiom of incongruence cannot itself belong to this primordial infinity. This is because the act of referencing it causes it to move beyond it. This movement occurs because the axiom ontologically separates this primordial infinity from truth. Inside the primordial infinity there is no truth; there exist no right or wrong answers. One can ask is X<5 and the answer will be yes, but the answer to the question does X=99 would also be yes. Separating truth from falsity in this infinity of information is futile and nonsensical. However, the axiom of incongruence still remains true. It appears to be the only true contingent statement that could be made about our hypothesized primordial infinity of information[13].

Therefore, due to its specificity and the inherent falsifiability that comes with it, the axiom of incongruence is "something", as opposed to the nothingness from which it arose. It is something which makes a statement about nothing. It therefore, no longer fits within the domain of nothing (the primordial infinity of information). It should exist in a new domain that we may now label "something". This axiom of incongruence would give rise to a second axiom that can be termed the axiom of consistency, which can be stated as: *in the domain of the axiom of incongruence (what we are now calling "something") there can be no incongruence.* This

---

[13] Of course necessary statements could be made about the primordial infinity of the nature that x=34 or y=9/x. However, these statements, by definition, could never be false. In contrast, the axiom of contraindication, while still an a priori truth, could be written in two forms. 1.) there are incongruent statements 2.) there are not any incongruent statements. One of them is true while the other is false. I am arguing that it is a contingent statement because its converse is falsifiable.

should be self-evident. If any incongruence between information statements existed, it would represent an immediate move back to the infinite primordial nothingness, which can also be termed the domain of incongruence. Therefore only information statements that are congruent with each other would conceptually fit in the domain of something. This could be the origin of the force of consistency, from which an information based physical reality could be constructed.

Of course I cannot empirically prove any of this or offer a logical argument any more rigorous than the one that I just attempted to make. This part of the book is admittedly speculation. However, it is interesting to note how much more workable the problem of creating physical existence is when one's task is merely to shuffle around information statements, axioms, and rules for organizing them as opposed to actually creating objectively existing physical beings out of nothing. It appears that the creation of reality is inherently more economical in idealism as compared to materialism. I think that this is one of many often overlooked conceptual benefits of idealism.

The Hard Problem of Idealism

But you may ask, where does consciousness come from? To which I would answer that it is fundamental, just as an adherent to materialism would say that elementary particles, or space-time, or strings are fundamental. As an idealist the real task is to explain the appearance of the physical world, or as I should say now the appearance of information. This is the hard problem of idealism: how does information keep getting created from temporal extensions of consciousness? This question is not difficult. Information is in a sense part of consciousness. While resisting a reduction to information consciousness is always about information. As time passes the existence of temporal extensions of consciousness tend to create larger and more complex entanglements, and it is through this process that they seem to be perpetually creating information.

Let us consider a mundane example. I am out on my porch and I am looking at my neighbor's driveway, the sun is out, and I hear the sounds of a party coming from the park down the street. They are playing *Billy Jean* by Michael Jackson. As this scene is unfolding the temporal extensions of my consciousness are making information. Information in its purest form is binary, comprised of yes or no answers to direct questions. Just by sitting on my porch for a few minutes an incalculable number of answers to such questions (an incalculable amount of information) can be generated. For example, I am looking at my neighbors' driveway. I see his red truck. That is a "yes" answer to the question, are your senses supplying you with the sensory input that you are surmising to be a red truck[14]. So far so simple, but wait. We must also consider the negative replies. Is there a white van in the driveway? No. Is there a purple Honda scooter? No. Are there any persons waving at me from the driveway? No. Are there any persons yelling at me from the drive way? No. Can I see any animal life at all in the driveway? No. This can go on ad infinitum

---

[14] For all of the upcoming examples, to be accurate, I would have to write a similarly awkward sentence of the form: are your senses supplying you with the sensory input that you are surmising to be a red truck. For clarity sake I am not going to do this, but I wanted to point it out.

for each of the five senses. Do I hear music? Yes. Is it Mozart? No. Is it the Beatles? No. Do I hear people talking? Yes. Do I hear a motorcycle engine? No. Do I hear a firecracker? No. Do I smell a decomposing body? No. Do I smell fresh cut grass? Yes. Do I smell burnt rubber? No. Do I smell bacon frying? No. Do I feel pain in my finger? No. Do I taste salt? No. Do I taste ice cream? No. Do I taste anything in my mouth? No.

In this way each temporal extension of consciousness creates a wealth of information. By forcing answers to questions (both yes and no) an incalculable multitude of bits of information are created by each and every temporal extension. This is the answer to the hard problem of idealism. Unlike the hard problem of materialism, the intractable problem of explaining how matter creates consciousness, the reverse of it, how consciousness creates information, seems undramatic and obvious. I would go as far as to say that the fact that idealism lacks a true "hard problem" should be considered a strong piece of evidence in its favor.

9

Empirical Approaches & Concluding Thoughts

How can naturalistic idealism be empirically validated? For certain there has been evidence in the past. The tests of the EPR paradox that demonstrate non-locality clearly support the notion that there is no space. Agreeing with Einstein's objections to this "spooky action at a distance", I find non-locality to be fundamentally at odds with the notion of a spatially extended physical reality. The problem, however, is that a critic could easily dismiss this as being completely post hoc. Since it is not a prediction that idealism had made first that it carries little weight. In other words, to assert in the 21st century that non-locality proves idealism is not nearly the same as asserting in 1890 that idealism is correct, and that it implies non-locality, and then articulating the EPR paradox along with Bell's inequalities, and correctly predicting subsequent experimental results. Therefore, in order to be taken seriously, the idealistic framework presented here will need to make some falsifiable future predictions.

I would like to start by making two negative predictions (i.e., predicting what will not happen). Although negative predictions are far easier to make than positive predictions, and do not carry as much weight in comparison, they are still falsifiable and an important part of science. For example, assume for a moment that we were living in the 18th century and someone proposed a theory that dinosaurs became extinct around 65 million years ago. A positive prediction would be that scientists will eventually be able to date the chemical compositions of dinosaur fossils and that we will find fossils that are older than 65 million years but none younger. Another positive prediction that one could make would be that one day we would find evidence of an astronomical cataclysm that could be dated to 65 million years ago. A negative prediction, in contrast, would be that humans, even in the most remote areas of the world, would never encounter any living dinosaurs. This negative prediction, although much easier to make than the positive ones, is still a completely falsifiable hypothesis. If we found a living tyrannosaurus the theory that dinosaurs have been extinct for 65 million years would instantly be proven false.

The first negative prediction that can be made from the perspective of naturalistic idealism is that the hard problem of consciousness will never be solved. By this I simply mean that a full explanation of human consciousness in terms of third person data will never be produced; that the ontological equivalence of consciousness and the motion of matter will never be demonstrated. Now we have to be careful here because for the last several decades more than a few philosophers and neuroscientists have been boldly claiming this very thing. Of course upon closer examination these theories tend to be more aptly described as potential pathways to an explanation rather than an explanation themselves. However, if neuroscience were ever to achieve this feat (not in principle but in actuality) that achievement would instantly render false the idealism presented here.

133

The second negative prediction that naturalistic idealism can make is that physicists will never develop an empirically validated theory of nonlocal hidden variables. The idealism presented here is predicated on a lack of objective realism. If somehow, in contrast to all previous evidence to the contrary, particles were ever shown to be able to hold on to the totality of their properties independent of measurement, that finding would also render false the idealism presented here.

In addition to these two negative predictions, naturalistic idealism can make three positive predictions. Of these, two can only be broadly defined at present, while the last can be formulated to a significant degree of specificity. The first broad prediction will be that physicists may one day find remote sections of the universe that have at least some properties that are currently existing in a superposition of possible states. When they measure these properties they will collapse these wave functions, and perhaps large sections of the cosmos will be changed by the particularities of the way the measurement occurred. The individuals who participate in this manipulation, by doing so, will wield god like power, likely over some insignificant factor but impressive all the same. But how can we determine that the effect was caused by the act of the observation and not by the fact that it was objectively existing this way independent of our observation? The answer may lie in some form of statistical experiment, where given an opportunity to repeat the manipulation by observation several times the results could be compared to what would have been expected by chance. By doing this repeatedly statistical evidence in favor of idealism may emerge.

Concluding Thoughts

The second broad prediction that can be made is that psychologists will someday find evidence for the universality of experience, the idea that pre reflective consciousness does not contain an "I". I do not have a clear idea on how this can be achieved. However it does not seem out of the range of possibility that this could be achieved through some, as yet unknown, experimental method that could deliver a falsifiable test.

The most specific positive prediction that naturalistic idealism can make is that experiments using the methods of cognitive psychology will provide evidence for the Consciousness Causes Collapse (CCC) interpretation of quantum mechanics. This result will nearly mandate idealism. Unlike the two other positive predictions that were made in this chapter, this prediction was able to be formulated to a much higher degree of specificity. It will therefore be presented in more detail.

Using Cognitive Psychology to Test Idealism

In cognitive psychology the term "priming" refers to an implicit memory effect where exposure to one stimulus influences a person's response time to another stimulus. For example, the word "Doctor" is recognized faster following the word "Nurse" than following "Table"; "Mother" is recognized faster following "Father" than following "Bread". Psychologists have been exploiting these reliable reaction time effects for decades as a multipurpose research tool. In recent years, these methods have even been used to prime subjects subliminally (Dehaene et al, 1998; Greenwald et al, 2003; Kouider & Dehaene, 2009). In such research subjects are flashed a stimulus (such as a word) on a computer screen for a length of time that is just underneath the duration that can be consciously experienced (about 50 milliseconds). Despite subjects reporting to not be aware of ever seeing the primed word, they demonstrated shorter reaction times responding to words that are semantically congruent with the primed word than they did responding to neutral words. Their brains had processed the meaning of the word and began to react to it even though they were not aware of it. The stimulus was processed unconsciously.

Unconscious semantic processing provides the mechanism through which it can be determined whether it is possible to document a wave function collapse prior to any interaction with consciousness. It appears to currently be possible for an interdisciplinary team of researchers to construct an experimental condition that, according to the Consciousness Causes Collapse (CCC) interpretation, would produce an unconscious semantic prime existing in a state of superposition. By measuring the differential effects that this uncollapsed and unconscious prime has on subjects' reaction time to semantically congruent words as opposed to control conditions researchers should be able to put the CCC interpretation to an empirical test.

The proposed experiment would require a physical devise that is set to measure a quantum phenomenon (e.g., particle spin, position) such that there is about a 50% chance that one of two outcomes would be obtained. These outcomes will be termed outcome A and outcome B. On each trial this physical measurement device will assess whether outcome A or outcome B occurred. This information would then be automatically uploaded into a computer that will briefly flash a word on a screen in front of an experimental subject for a length of time that they would be able to process unconsciously but be underneath the length of time needed to be consciously experienced. One of two (semantically incongruent) words will be flashed depending on which outcome was registered in the physical measurement devise. The subject would then be asked to make a rapid response to another verbal stimulus. This stimulus will be specially chosen to be semantically incongruent with the prime presented on the occurrence of outcome A and congruent with the prime presented on the occurrence of outcome B. Multiple trials will be completed with each subject. A different set of words will be used for each trial. The subject's response time for each trial will be recorded. Based on past research in cognitive psychology it would be expected that the primed words (even though they are flashed for a length of time too short to be experienced consciously) would affect the subject's reaction times where it would take them less time to respond to semantically congruent words than it will to respond to semantically incongruent words. Pre experimental work will be required such that the experimental apparatus related to the subliminal priming, reaction time measurements, and semantically congruent word pairings are consistently succeeding in obtaining this outcome.

Each subject will be run through a number of trials alternating between the experimental and control conditions on a predetermined randomized sequence. The only difference between the experimental and the control condition will be the time at which the experimenter takes a reading of the physical measurement devise.

Control Condition: In the control condition the experimenter will view the read out of the physical measurement devise before the subject is shown the prime.

Experimental Condition: In the experimental condition the experimenter will view the read out of the physical measurement devise only after the subject has responded to the prime[15].

Hypothesis: If the CCC interpretation is correct, priming effects should be found in the control condition but not in the experimental condition. If the CCC is not correct then priming effects should be found in both the control and the experimental conditions.

According to the CCC interpretation of quantum mechanics not just the particles being measured but the physical measurement device itself and related physical systems exist in a state of superposition until they come into contact with consciousness. It is only at that point does the wave function collapse and one of the possibilities is realized. If this view is correct, then in the proposed experiment the collapse of the wave function will not occur until the experimenter looks at the read out from the physical measurement devise. This would be the first time that the outcome of the measurement would have interacted with consciousness. In the control condition this occurs before the unconscious primes are given and the subject is asked

---

[15] It is of paramount importance that no information regarding the outcome of the quantum measurement come into contact with anyone in anyway before the appointed time. If this occurs the experiment would be invalidated.

to respond to them. In this condition the primes should have the expected effect on the subjects' reaction times. In contrast, the experimental condition requires the experimenter to wait to observe the read out on the measurement devise until after the subject responds to the unconscious primes. In this condition, according to the CCC, the primes should still be in a state of superposition when they are being processed by the subject's unconscious neural pathways, themselves also in a state of superposition. Because they are in superposition the primes should cancel each other out, or possibly have some other nonsensical effect. The expected priming effects should not occur.

After data is collected from multiple subjects who each participated in multiple trials that are systematically varied between the two conditions the results should be clear. Either the primes work in the experimental condition or they do not. If the primes work in the control condition but not the experimental condition, it would seem that the only explanation could be that they existed in superposition when processed by the subjects. This would mean that, consistent with the CCC interpretation, the experimenter produced a macro superposition encompassing not only the physical measuring devise itself but another computer along with the neural activity in a human brain. The result would indicate that it is the interaction with consciousness itself as opposed to either the physical measurement devise or unconscious neural processes that triggered the collapse of the wave function. Such a finding would be fatal to the assumption of objective realism. The blow would be far more fundamental than what was found in previous experimental work (e.g., Aspect, 1999;

Gröblacher et al, 2007) because it would indicate that physical reality bends not to the state of a human made measurement devise but directly to subjective experience itself. The other potential result would be that the primes would work equally well in both conditions. This result would suggest that consciousness itself has nothing to do with the collapse of the wave function. Such a finding would appear to deal a fatal blow to the idealism presented here.

Embracing Idealism

If ontology is to be regarded as the search for the ultimate truth then there is no need for philosophers to argue their case using pragmatics. Reality either works this way or it does not. Maybe empirical methods will one day clarify the issue and maybe they will not. Maybe the materialists are correct and the entire forgoing should be viewed as an elaborate fabrication based on a colossal error. However, what if the foregoing was true and this truth was eventually recognized? What would be the implications? What can we speculate? Just for fun.

Perhaps the most obvious implication would be that an embrace of idealism would lay the framework for vast improvements to the science of psychology. Being a psychologist one might find it strange that I have talked so little about my own scientific discipline. Let me try and remedy that neglect here. As I mentioned earlier psychology has no place for consciousness. Everything in psychology is focused on the essence of mental concepts, everything is abstractions. The content of human experiences themselves, the phenomenology, has been expelled from the science. This may have been for good reason in the early to middle twentieth century, as it has allowed for tremendous progress in understanding basic psychological processes, cognitive and emotional development, personality, and psychopathology. However, we may soon be reaching the point where such a bare bones approach may no longer be the most productive strategy. Our research paradigms appear to be yielding diminishing returns. An embrace of idealism would focus psychology on what should be its primary subject, consciousness itself.

A psychology based in idealism may help usher in an era where we could more rapidly advance the treatment of emotional and behavioral disorders, an era where knowledge of our basic cognitive and emotional processes could grow by leaps and bounds. I will admit that I do not have a clue on how any of this could be accomplished. I do not see the specifics of that path going forward. However, what I am saying, with certainty, is that an embrace of idealism would stand the discipline of psychology on its head. It would require us to radically reframe every single problem in the field. It would mandate an entirely different perspective. Such a Copernican revolution has the potential to spark advancements that have never before been dreamed. The yield could be tremendous.

In addition to transforming psychology, seriously embracing idealism could offer the possibility for magnificent technological advancements. The idealism presented here is predicated on the Consciousness Causes Collapse Interpretation of quantum mechanics being correct. If and when this proves to be the case, many researchers in various fields may choose to embrace it, regardless of their philosophy, because of the promise for gigantic technological leaps. Manipulating superpositions and macro entanglements by choosing when and how to make observations has the potential to yield "god like" power over the natural world. We are not there yet, and again, I am not sure of exactly how this would be accomplished. But the potential definitely exists, even if I am unable to articulate the specifics. To defend my ignorance, I would point out that many forward looking scientists in 1850 would have been able to see the great technological potential that harnessing the power of electricity would bring, even though they might not yet of understood the specifics of how to make a light bulb, a toaster, or a radio. Similarly, the early pioneers of computing in the middle 20th century could foresee the great potential of digital technology without actually being able to engineer a 21st century mobile devise. In the same way, although I cannot yet describe the workings of such a future technology, I can see that it has vast potential, one that could possibly yield a higher degree of technological progress than either the harnessing of electricity or the development of digital computing.

Thirdly, an embrace of naturalistic idealism will drastically alter how we view ourselves and our place in the universe. It will reverse the steady downgrade in importance that humanity has suffered over the last 500 years. Until the renaissance and the later birth of science humans thought that they existed in the center of the universe. The earth was only thought to be as old as recorded history. Humans had a direct relationship with God, the creator of all reality. We were so important that even our daily transgressions were significant enough to command his attention and anger.

In 1543 Nicolaus Copernicus published his master

work *On the Revolutions of the Heavenly Spheres* where he outlined his helio centric theory of the solar system. Never again would the earth be thought of as the center of the universe, only as an insignificant cog in a larger solar system. Then, in 1859 Charles Darwin publishes *On the Origin of Species* and deals humanity a down grade much more significant than that of Copernicus. With the theory of evolution the creation of humans becomes an accident of chance as opposed to a deliberate act. Humanity is knocked off its pedestal at the zenith of creation, and we are regulated to the most recent occurrence on a particular branch of the evolutionary tree, no different in importance than the modern house fly or rose bush. Then, we learned that the earth is billions of years old rather than just six thousand. With a young earth every bit of its existence was at least filled with the great deeds of human history. But with our recorded history being just a tiny speck compared to the biological history and even larger pre biological history of earth, humanity finds itself without a central importance in the history of our own planet. It continues to get worse. Until the twentieth century we thought that our universe was indeed our galaxy. Now we see it as only one of at least a 100 billion other galaxies, each holding within themselves billions of stars. These mind boggling numbers make Copernicus's diminution of earth seem downright trivial. Lastly, much closer to home, eliminative materialism in the 20th and 21st century philosophy of mind (e.g., Ryle, Dennett) attacked the reality of our subjective consciousness itself, contending that it is mere illusion. In essence not only are we insignificant in the scope of the broader universe, and not only is our evolution an unintended accident of random chance, but our conscious reality itself is not as real as we believe it to be. Thus we have even lost the dignity of our own minds.

The naturalistic idealism presented here is a complete reversal of that trend towards insignificance. The obvious conclusion is that it elevates humanity (along with other conscious beings) to a place of central importance in reality. This may have both positive and negative consequences.

Lastly, embracing naturalistic idealism could lead to the recognition of the universality of experience. Put simply, we are not as alone as it seems. Without space there is no separation. Our temporal extensions of consciousness are stacked up by the billions on top of each other in time. To say that all lives are lived would be an over simplification but it would not be entirely incorrect. In a sense there is only one (nonspecific) consciousness, and that consciousness manifests itself through different biological lenses, so that your experiences are manifestations of the underlying psychic ether that underwrites reality. For the common person, this realization could represent a powerful reorientation from the individual toward the collective. This potential societal change may dwarf any technological benefit that may be simultaneously reaped.

Of course Buddhism has been expounding a similar view for millennia, that reality has a wholeness to it, and this has not lead to any great peace in the areas where it was prominent. Even the monotheistic religions in the west contain a similar love thy neighbor sentiment. Unfortunately, this too has not lead to peace. However, there is a thread in both of these traditions that differs from the naturalistic idealism presented here. In Buddhism, as I understand it, beings are reincarnated after death to a higher or lower place based upon how they lived their life. The spiritual rewards and punishments are tied to an individual spirit. The same concept exists in Christianity, Islam, and Judaism where one's soul is eternally bound for either hell or heaven depending on how you lived, or what you believed. Again the rewards and punishments are tied to your individual spirit, your soul. In contrast, although it can be easily be interpreted through a traditional religious lens, taken at face value naturalistic idealism suggests that there are not billions of individual souls connected to billions of biological bodies, but rather that there is one consciousness that has expression through billions of biological bodies. In naturalistic idealism that awareness never ends. It continues to exist in others, just as it is doing right now. Therefore, ultimate happiness lies not in keeping your soul pious, but in making others happy. This is the prima fascia consequence of this idealism.

Conclusion

In the final analysis I find that I am asking myself whether I actually believe what I have written. Doing so is an unsettling activity. After some time wrestling with this I realized this was the wrong question to be asking. If one ponders philosophy long and deep enough they travel so far from everyday notions of things that all the metaphysical options start to sound "crazy". Nothing at all sounds obviously true. Therefore, the important question is not whether I believe with absolute certainty in everything that I have written, but in what I find more likely to be true, idealism or materialism. Framed in this way, I can attest that I have no faith in materialism whatsoever. I would find it hard to even fake it. It is this that compels me to embrace idealism, and to struggle to improve upon its previous articulations. If I had to bet my life on it, I would be absolutely confident in the essesential nature of matter and energy, and I would also be absolutely confident in the idea that the reason consciousness does not fit easily within a physical framework is because its nature is to escape its essence through its being over time. I would also be confident, although to a lesser degree, with the proposed mechanism of mental causation, the contention of the universality of experience, and the conclusions regarding free will. On the other hand I am only marginally confident with my cosmological speculations and the possibility that idealism would result in significant improvements to the science of psychology in the foreseeable future.

Of course, in the ultimate analysis my confidence level is completely irrelevant. The entire forgoing could be completely true or it could be completely false. It could also be only partially true. Maybe the parts in which I am the most confident are the parts that are based on the biggest errors, and the parts in which I have less confidence are true for reasons that I have completely overlooked. Unlike religion and politics, proper philosophy and proper science are achieved by unyielding skepticism, even if that means being skeptical of your own skepticism.

In the end I find idealism to be the only intellectually honest metaphysical solution. If the details of the ontological framework presented here turn out to be incorrect (e.g., temporal extensions of consciousness, existential / essesential being, the force of consistency, the division/unity of consciousness, mental causation, the cosmological speculations) that does not prove that idealism is not correct, rather that only the idealism presented here is immature and incomplete, which I am sure that it is in many ways. Scientifically responsible idealistic thought that respects the empirical facts of physics, biology, and psychology is in its infancy; more accurately, it has not even been born yet. It needs to be developed, worked on. It is my hope that serious naturalistically minded individuals will continue to develop and refine idealistic ontologies. For the past several hundred years there have been literally millions of scientists and philosophers in the world that subscribe to materialism. The weight of their work is vast, and their overwhelming consensus gives the impression that the issue has been definitively settled. But this is not true. The issue has not been settled. Remember that there is, and always will be, room for doubt.

Appendix

This book endeavored to present two related theses, one broad and one specific. The broad thesis is the general contention that idealism is the correct metaphysical position, the one that corresponds to the reality in which we inhabit. The specific thesis is that the idealistic ontology presented here is an accurate articulation of the workings of the reality in which we inhabit. Needless to say the broad thesis is more likely to be true than the specific one. Although narrative text allows writers to fill in necessary details and add color to their points, at times it can also lead to a lack of clarity regarding the pillars of an argument. Therefore, I thought that it would be helpful to break down both the general argument for idealism and the argument for the specific ontology presented in this book, (i.e., naturalistic idealism) in the shortest form possible.

A Three Statement Summary of the Evidence for Idealism in General

1.) The prima fascia evidence for consciousness being fundamental is greater than the evidence that matter is fundamental. We know of consciousness' fundamentality because we know it directly, while we can only infer the reality of matter. One is beyond doubt while the other appears to be an unprovable proposition.

2.) The philosophy literature contains several strong arguments for the fundamentality of consciousness, however there are no such arguments asserting the fundamentality of matter (i.e., physical reality. In other words, the many arguments in the materialist literature are offensive arguments against the fundamentality of consciousness; they do not do the work of defending the fundamentality of matter. The fundamentality of matter is simply assumed to be true. Taken in total, although most philosophers subscribe to materialism, there is more direct philosophical evidence for consciousness being fundamental than matter being fundamental.

3.) There are unsought empirical findings from quantum mechanics that appear to strip matter of its objective presence outside of measurement. If we equate measurement with consciousness experience of measurement then we arrive at the doorstep to idealism. The only other way to get around this is to subscribe to the many worlds hypothesis, which appears to be far less parsimonious of an answer than idealism. By comparison, as long as you are ready to remove any *a priori* prejudices against consciousness having a place in the foundation of reality, idealism and the consciousness causes collapse interpretation of quantum mechanics is downright conservative.

Appendix

A Four Statement Summary of Naturalistic Idealism

1.) Due to their internal homogeneity and indistinguishability, the elementary particles that comprise the matter and energy of the physical universe can hold on to no being apart from their essence; they exist solely as information, having no independent objective persistence through time. The superposition of quantum phenomenon in between measurements is the logical consequence of this.

2.) Unlike elementary particles whose existence is completely contained within their essence, each individual temporal extension of consciousness is an example of existential being, a being that can escape its own essence, a being that exists beyond it. This is what separates consciousness ontologically from matter. Physical things exist only as essence, while temporal extensions of consciousness exist beyond their essence through their irreducibility and being over time.

3.) All co-occurring, and otherwise related, temporal extensions of consciousness comprise a super entanglement where each one must hold an equally valid claim on accuracy of their perspective. Consistency within this entanglement is the fundamental ontological force and is always maintained. This entanglement between consciousness and information forms reality.

4.) The reliability and the immutable nature of physical laws stem from this reality wide entanglement, not from the existential presence of physical structures persisting independently in time. Therefore, the primary causal force in the universe (consistency in entanglement) is teleological rather than mechanistic in nature.

Bibliography

Allport, D. A. (1968). Phenomenal Simultaneity and the Perceptual Moment Hypothesis. *British Journal of Psychology, 59*(4), 395-406.

Aspect, A. (1999) Bell's inequality test: more ideal than ever, *Nature 398*, 189-190.

Aspect, A., Dalibard, J. & Roger, G. (1982) Experimental test of Bell's inequalities using time-varying analyzers. *Physical Review Letters, 49*, 1804-1807.

Aspect, A, Grangier, P. & Roger, G. (1981). Experimental tests of realistic local theories via Bell's theorem. *Physical Review Letters, 47,* 460-463.

Ballentine, L. E. (1970). The Statistical Interpretation of Quantum Mechanics. *Review of Modern Physics 42*, 358.

Beck, F. & Eccles, J. C. (1998). "Quantum processes in the brain: A scientific basis of consciousness". *Cognitive Studies: Bulletin of the Japanese Cognitive Science Society 5* (2): 95–109.

Bergson, H. (1910). *Time and Free Will: An Essay on the Immediate Data of Consciousness*, tr., F.L. Pogson, Montana: Kessinger Publishing.

Bell, J. (1964). On the Einstein Podolsky Rosen Paradox. *Physics 1* (3): 195–200.

Bohm, D. (1952). A suggested interpretation of the quantum theory in terms of hidden variables. *Physical Review, 85* 166–179.

Bostrom, N. (2003). Are you living in a computer simulation? *Philosophical Quarterly, Vol. 53,* No. 211, pp. 243-255.

Bradley, F. H. (1893). *Appearance and Reality.* London: S. Sonnenschein; New York: Macmillan.

Broad, C. D. (1925). *The Mind and Its Place in Nature*, London: Kegan Paul.

Chalmers, D. (1995). Facing up to the problem of consciousness. *Journal of Consciousness Studies, 2* (3), 200-219.

Chalmers, D. (1996). *The Conscious Mind: In Search of a Fundamental Theory.* New York: Oxford University Press.

Chalmers, D. (2010*). The Character of Consciousness.* New York: Oxford University Press.

Churchland, PM and Churchland, P.S., (1998). *On the Contrary: Critical Essays 1987-1997.* Cambridge, Massachusetts: The MIT Press

Descartes, R., Weissman, D., & Bluhm, W. T. (1996). *Discourse on the method; and, Meditations on first philosophy.* New Haven: Yale University Press.

Bibliography

Dehaene, S. (2014). *Consciousness and the Brain: Deciphering How the Brain Codes Our Thoughts.* Viking Adult, New York.

Dehaene, S., Naccache, L., Le Clec', H., Koechlin, E., Mueller, M., Dehaene-Lambertz, G., Van De Moortele, P. F., Le Bihan, D. (1998). Imaging unconscious seman tic priming. *Nature 395* (6702): 597–600.

Dennett, D. C. (1991). *Consciousness Explained.* Boston: Little, Brown and Company.

D'Espagnat, B. (1979). "The Quantum Theory and Reality," *Scientific American,* 241:158.

Deutsch, D. (1999). Quantum Theory of Probability and Decisions. *Proceedings of the Royal Society of London* A455, 3129–3137.

De Witt, B. S. M. (1970). 'Quantum mechanics and Reality', *Physics Today,* 23(9): 30–35.

Einstein, A., Podolsky, B., & Rosen, N. (1935). Can the quantum-mechanical description of physical reality be considered complete? *Physical Review,.* 47, 777.

Everett, H., (1957). Relative State' Formulation of Quantum Mechanics, *Reviews of Modern Physics,* 29: 454–462.

Feigl, H. (1958). The 'mental' and the 'physical'. *Minnesota Studies in the Philosophy of Science* 2:370-497.

155

Fingelkurts, A. A., & Fingelkurts, A. A. (2006). Timing in cognition and EEG brain dynamics: discreteness versus continuity. *Cognitive Processing, 7*, 135–162.

Flanagan, O. (2003). *The Problem Of The Soul: Two Visions of Mind and How To Reconcile Them*. New York: Basic Books.

Friedman, J.R., Patel, V., Chen, W., Tolpygo, S.K., Lukens, J.E. (2000). Quantum superposition of distinct macroscopic states, *Nature 406*: 43–46.

French, S., (2007). 'Identity and individuality in quantum theory,' The Stanford Encyclopedia of Philosophy, Edward N. Zalta, ed.

Goswami, A. (1993). *The Self-Aware Universe*. New York: Putnam's Sons.

Greenwald, A. G., Abrams, R. L., Naccache, L., & Dehaene, S. (2003). Long-term semantic memory versus contextual memory in unconscious number processing. *Journal of Experimental Psychology: Learning, Memory, and Cognition, 29*, 235–247.

Griffiths, R. (1984). Consistent histories and the interpret tation of quantum mechanics. *Journal of Statistical Physics, 36*, 219–272.

Gröblacher, S., Paterek, T., Kaltenbaek, R., Brukner, C., Zukowski, M., Aspelmeyer, M. (2007). An experimental test of non-local realism. *Nature, 446*(7138), 871-875.

Bibliography

Heidegger, M. (1962). *Being and Time*. Oxford: Blackwell.

Herzon, M. H., Kammer, T. Scharnowksi. F. (2016). Time Slices: What Is the Duration of a Percept? *http://dx.doi.org/10.1371/journal.pbio.1002433*

Hodgson, D. (2005). A Plain Person's Free Will. *Journal of Consciousness Studies 12(1) 1-19*.

Hoffman, D. (2007). Conscious Realism and the Mind-Body Problem. *Mind & Matter Vol. 6*(1), pp. 87–121.

Jackson, F. (1982). "Epiphenomenal Qualia". *Philosophical Quarterly* 32: 127–136.

Jackson, F. (1986). "What Mary Didn't Know". *Journal of Philosophy* 83: 291–295.

Jackson, F. (2011). Philosophy Bites podcast, Frank Jackson on What Mary Knew. url: http://philosophybites. com/201108/frank-jackson-on-what-mary-knew.html

James, W. (1912). *Essays in Radical Empiricism*. New York: Longmans, Green, and Co.

Jeans, J., H. (1930). *The Mysterious Universe*. Cambridge University Press (reissued by Cambridge University Press, 2009)

Johnston, M. (1997), 'How to Speak of the Colors', in (Byrne, A. & Hilbert, D. (eds.) *Readings on Color. Volume 1: The Philosophy of Color*, Cambridge and London, MIT Press., pp. 137-172.

Kant, I., & Meiklejohn, J. M. (1901). *Critique of pure reason.* New York: P.F. Collier and Son.

Kouider, S., & Dehaene, S. (2009). Subliminal number priming within and across the visual and auditory modalities. *Experimental Psychology, 56(6)*, 418-433.

Kripke, S. (1981). *Naming and Necessity,* Oxford, Basil Blackwell.

Lakoff, G., & Johnson, M. (1999). *Philosophy in the flesh: The embodied mind and its challenge to western thought.* Basic books.

Lanza, R., & Berman, B. (2009). *Biocentrism.* Dallas: BenBella.

Levine, J. (1983). Materialism and Qualia: The Explanatory Gap. *Pacific Philosophical Quarterly 64*, 354-361.

Levine, J. 2001. *Purple Haze: The Puzzle of Conscious Experience.* Cambridge, Mass: The MIT Press

Lewis, D., 1983, Postscript to "Mad Pain and Martian Pain", in D. Lewis, *Philosophical Papers* (Volume 1), Oxford: Oxford University Press.

Bibliography

Loar, B., 1990, "Phenomenal States" (Revised Version), in *The Nature of Consciousness: Philosophical Debates*, N. Block, O. Flanagan, G. Güzeldere (eds.), Cambridge, MA: MIT Press, 1997.

McGinn, C. (1989). Can we solve the Mind-Body Problem? In *Mind 98*: 349-66.

Nagel, T. (1974). "What Is It Like to Be a Bat?", *The Philosophical Review*, Vol. 83, 4, 435-450.

Nemirow, L. (2007). So this is what it's like: a defense of the ability hypothesis, in T. Alter & S. Walter: *Phenomenal Concepts and Phenomenal Knowledge. New Essays on Consciousness and Physicalism*, Oxford: Oxford University Press.

Papineau, D. (2002). *Thinking about Consciousness*. Oxford: Oxford University Press.

Penrose, R. (1999) [1989], *The Emperor's New Mind* (New Preface (1999)ed.), Oxford, England: Oxford University Press.

Place, U.T. (1956). Is Consciousness a Brain Process?, *British Journal of Psychology, 47*: 44–50.

Rey, G. "A Question About Consciousness." In N. Block, O. Flanagan, and G. Güzeldere eds. *The Nature of Consciousness*. Cambridge, MA: MIT Press, 461-482, 1997.

Rovelli, C. (1996). "Relational quantum mechanics", International *Journal of Theoretical Physics, 35* 1637–1678.

Russell, B. (1912). *The problems of philosophy.* New York: Holt.

Russell, B. (1921). *The Analysis of Mind.* London, G. Allen & Unwin; New York, Macmillan.

Ryle G. (1949). *Concept of Mind.* University of Chicago Press.

Sartre, J. P. (1953). *Being and nothingness.* New York: Washington Square Press.

Sartre, J. P. (1936/2004). *The Transcendence of the Ego: A sketch for a phenomenological description.* Routledge.

Schlosshauer, M., Koer J., Zeilinger, A. (2013). A Snap shot of Foundational Attitudes Toward Quantum Mechanics. *Studies in History and Philosophy of Science Part B: Studies in History and Philosophy of Modern Physics 44* (3): 222–230.

Schwartz, J.M. & Begley, S. (2002). *The Mind and The Brain.* New York: Harper Collins.

Searle, John R. (1997). *The Mystery of Consciousness.* Granta Books.

Bibliography

Smart, J.J.C. 1959. "Sensations and Brain Processes."
Reprinted in *Materialism and the Mind-Body Problem*, ed. D.
Rosenthal. Indianapolis: Hackett, 1987.

Stapp, H. P. (1993/2003). *Mind, matter, and quantum
mechanics*. New York: Springer-Verlag.

Stapp, H. P. (2005). Quantum Interactive Dualism: An
Alternative to Materialism. *Journal of Consciousness Studies*
12 (11), 43-58.

Stroud, J. M. (1955). The fine structure of psychological
time. In: Quastler H (ed). Information theory in psy
chology: problems and methods. The Free Press, Glen
coe, Ill, pp 174–205.

Tegmark, M. (2008). The Mathematical Universe.
Foundations of Physics, 38:101-150.

Tegmark, M. (2014). *Our Mathematical Universe: My
Quest for the Ultimate Nature of Reality*. New York:
Random House.

Tittel, W. J., Brendel, H. Zbinden, N. Gisin (1998), "Vio
lation of Bell inequalities by photons more than 10 km
apart", *Physical Review Letters* 81: 3563–6.

Ursin, F., (2007). Entanglement-based quantum com-
munication over 144 km. *Nature physics 3* (7), 481-486.

VanRullen, R., & Koch, C. (2003). Is perception discrete or continuous? *Trends in Cognitive Science, 7,* 201-213.

Von Neumann, J. 1955/1932: *Mathematical Foundations of Quantum Mechanics.* Princeton: Princeton University Press. (Translated by Robert T. Beyer from the 1932 German original, Mathematiche Grundlagen der Quantummechanik. Berlin: J. Springer

Walker, E. H. (1998). Quantum theory of consciousness. *Noetic Journal, 1,* 100-107.

Weihs, G., Jennewein, T., Simon, C., Weinfurter, H. & Zeilinger, A. (1998). Violation of Bell's inequality under strict Einstein locality conditions. *Physical Review Letters, 81,* 5039-5043.

Wheeler, J. A. (1990). Information, physics, quantum: The search for links. In Zurek, Wojciech Hubert. *Complexity, Entropy, and the Physics of Information.* Redwood City, California: Addison-Wesle.

Wigner, E. P. (1961). Remarks on the mind-body ques tion. In I. J. Good (Ed.), *The scientist speculates.* Lon don: Heinemann.